T0112882

"Borderline personality disorder (BPD), which can be difficult for clinicians to manage, can also be painful for families and loved ones. They need help to avoid conflict and to respond in helpful ways. This book, written in highly accessible language, provides many practical tips on communicating about intense emotions and understanding troubled people."

—**Joel Paris, MD**, professor in the department of psychiatry at McGill University, and author of *Treatment of Borderline Personality Disorder*

"Those who struggle to keep the peace with difficult people in their daily lives will find these explanations and strategies extremely informative and helpful. You can be effective, and Jerold Kreisman will show you how!"

—**Sandy Hotchkiss, PsyD, LCSW**, author of *Why Is It Always About You?*

"For anyone who loves, lives with, or must care for a person struggling with BPD, Jerold Kreisman has written another useful guide full of empathic and pragmatic techniques. All too often, interactions with these individuals prove to be confusing, painful, and sometimes infuriating; Kreisman outlines a detailed approach for coping and keeping your head. As a clinician who has worked with individuals who suffer from this disorder, as well as the people who know them, I found his guidance to harmonize with my own experience and to echo the advice I often give to my own clients."

—**Joseph Burgo, PhD**, psychotherapist, *Psychology Today* blogger, and author of *The Narcissist You Know*, *Why Do I Do That?*, and the forthcoming *Shame*

"The lessons in respectful listening and mindful speech offered by this book will serve a broad audience. Ultimately, everyone struggles—to some degree or another—to understand and be understood. My commitment to feminist critiques of psychiatric categories leads me to be cautious around diagnostic terminology that labels one person in a conflict as disordered, but with that caveat in mind, I think of this book as an instruction in the 'humble warrior' pose of difficult conversations, as it advocates strength, balance, and grace in communicating with clients and loved ones who experience heightened interpersonal sensitivities. I can't think of qualities more necessary in the current moment than those modeled here by Kreisman: support, empathy, truth, understanding, and perseverance."

> —**Merri Lisa Johnson**, professor of women's and gender studies at USC Upstate, and author of *Girl in Need of a Tourniquet*

"*Talking to a Loved One with Borderline Personality Disorder* is a much-needed book for loved ones of someone with BPD, as well as for psychotherapists. I've had many clients throughout my forty years as a therapist who are at their wits' end when it comes to knowing how to communicate with a BPD loved one without the conversation escalating into an argument. Kreisman presents effective strategies to help readers learn how to communicate in the best way possible to ensure that they are heard, and their loved one doesn't feel humiliated or blamed. I will recommend this book to many of my clients and colleagues."

> —**Beverly Engel, LMFT**, author of *It Wasn't Your Fault*

"If somebody you care about struggles with BPD, this book will change your relationship with them forever! In this well-crafted guide, Jerold Kreisman masterfully describes the unique communication challenges this disorder produces and offers practical, step-by-step examples of how to deal with them effectively. You will think someone has been eavesdropping on your conversations! If your desire is to better connect with a loved one in your life with BPD and save yourself future emotional exhaustion in the process, it is unlikely that you will find a better resource."

—**Jeff Riggenbach, PhD,** president at the CBT Institute
of Oklahoma, and author of *Borderline Personality
Disorder Toolbox*

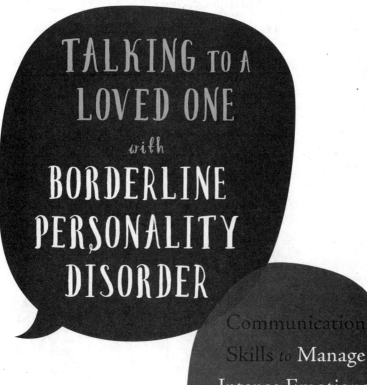

TALKING TO A LOVED ONE

with

BORDERLINE PERSONALITY DISORDER

Communication Skills *to* Manage Intense Emotions, Set Boundaries & Reduce Conflict

Jerold J. Kreisman, MD

New Harbinger Publications, Inc.

Publisher's Note

This publication is designed to provide accurate and authoritative information in regard to the subject matter covered. It is sold with the understanding that the publisher is not engaged in rendering psychological, financial, legal, or other professional services. If expert assistance or counseling is needed, the services of a competent professional should be sought.

NEW HARBINGER PUBLICATIONS is a
registered trademark of New Harbinger Publications, Inc.

Distributed in Canada by Raincoast Books

Copyright © 2018 by Jerold J. Kreisman
New Harbinger Publications, Inc.
5674 Shattuck Avenue
Oakland, CA 94609
www.newharbinger.com

Cover design by Amy Shoup

Acquired by Jess O'Brien

Edited by Cindy B. Nixon

All Rights Reserved

Library of Congress Cataloging-in-Publication Data on file

Printed in the United States of America.

24   23   22

10   9   8   7   6   5

For the little ones,
who grew to be the big ones,
who care for the next little ones:

Jenny and Adam

Alicia and Brett

Audrey and Owen

Stella and Ryder

Contents

Foreword

You can find tools and principles for effective communication in any relationship book. Communication isn't about proving you're right, but about respecting your partner's point of view. Actively listen—don't just talk. Put yourself in the other person's shoes. Be mindful in your words and tone. Tell your partner what you appreciate about them. Be willing to say "I'm sorry."

But what if one member of the couple has borderline personality disorder (BPD), and sometimes has trouble doing *all* these things? People with BPD may have lots of empathy for other people, but when emotionally aroused, they can go into attack mode. When a partner asks them to be accountable for their actions, or to speak differently (implying they were doing it wrong before), things may get even worse. Eventually, the non-borderline person may only talk to their partner when they have to. The relationship dies.

Is there any hope of bringing the two of you together to really problem-solve? Yes. There really is. Here's a metaphor for what's in store. Around the time of the Civil War, two competitive companies were hired to build the transcontinental railroad. One would start in Omaha and race west; the other would begin in San Francisco and head east. Together, they aimed to do the impossible: get two railroads to meet in the exact same place so the final rails fit together perfectly. It took forever to plan. But finally, when everybody was good and ready, they started. They blasted their way through granite mountains and laid track in passes smothered in eighteen feet of snow.

A meeting of the minds; a meeting of the railroads. Both happening in trackless countries where it's easy to get lost. One party walks on eggshells through emotional dangers; the other works through towering snow drifts and other physical hazards. It's too late for the railway men to do anything different—their time is past. *But it's not too late for you and your borderline loved one!* The psychiatrist who will help you learn to navigate treacherous discussions *together* is Jerry Kreisman. *Talking to a Loved One with Borderline Personality Disorder* is a brilliant book that you will find yourself rereading again and again.

Let's start with a very brief look at his method. Dr. Kreisman introduced the SET (support-empathy-truth) communications technique in his first book, *I Hate You—Don't Leave Me* (1989). It became quite popular—many people still use it today. Over the next thirty years of working with clients, Dr. Kreisman refined and expanded SET to a whole other level—like taking it from an old-timey bicycle (big wheel in front, little one in back) to the latest Harley-Davidson motorcycle.

Today, SET-UP (the UP stands for *understanding* and *perseverance*) is more than just a communication system. It's an essential tool for improving the relationship itself—because effective, respectful discussions are at the heart of building trust and love.

SET-UP is an extremely clear and practical method. Using it, you can keep a discussion on track, and when you and your partner go off the rails, you can pinpoint when things went wrong and correct them. In *Talking to a Loved One with Borderline Personality Disorder,* Dr. Kreisman uses dozens of examples, so it all sinks in. It's a lovely thing that the book is so very easy to read. You don't need to wrestle with any BPD jargon; it is just powerful, practical, road-tested help.

In the first three chapters, Dr. Kreisman explains the basics of the SET-UP system. In the rest of the book, he shows you how to use it in several dilemmas that are common in BPD relationships:

the no-win dilemma; the "I hate you" dilemma; the fear-of-being-abandoned dilemma; the no-identity dilemma; the "I'm a victim" dilemma; the impulsive self-destruction dilemma; and even the "should stay or should I go" dilemma.

Does the prospect of better communications—and a better relationship—sound improbable? So was the meeting of the rail-roads at Promontory Summit, Utah Territory, where they had a ceremony for the driving of the last spike on May 10, 1869, celebrating the completion of the first Transcontinental Railroad.

Go read the book now. It's time to get started.

—Randi Kreger, author of *Stop Walking on Eggshells* and *The Essential Family Guide to Borderline Personality Disorder*

Acknowledgments

When one puts words to screen and embarks on producing work that he hopes will be engaging and prove helpful, there is always a team around urging him on. They encourage, critique, and tolerate. My team has been a truly dedicated squad.

At New Harbinger, Jess O'Brien initially ignited my enthusiasm and kept close and comforting watch through the process. Editors Nicola Skidmore and Clancy Drake and copy editor Cindy Nixon guided me on my straight but sometimes not-so-narrow path. All chaperoned me graciously throughout the process.

My family's forbearance was indispensable. When it would always have been so much more fun to be with them, they encouraged me to close the door and stare at the computer a bit longer. My kids, grandkids, and, as in all things, my wife, Judy, helped me make deadlines and still have time for our adventures together.

I am indebted to my teachers and colleagues, whose wisdom and experience continue to inspire me. I am grateful most of all to my patients, my most important instructors. They guide me in useful directions and gently redirect me from my missteps. They entrust their care to me and allow me to collaborate with their explorations. I strive to deserve the courage they display to me and the trust with which they endow me.

Introduction

If you love someone with borderline personality disorder (BPD), you already know that the relationship can often be strained. You know that your loved one can exhibit changeable moods, impulsive behaviors, and even self-defeating activities that challenge your commitment. He may express anger that pushes you away, then desperately cling to you, demanding that you pull him closer. He may express adoration beyond measure, alternating with contempt beyond reason. She may be your lover or your best friend. She may be your parent or your child.

This work is an attempt to present practical ways to navigate these sometimes turbulent waters. It is intended to help you understand your loved one's often perplexing communication patterns, avoid the pitfalls, and develop ways to connect more positively.

Unlike many other works on the subject, this reference is not necessarily intended for those diagnosed with BPD, nor is it meant to explicate or replace a formal, professional treatment regimen. It is directed specifically at those who are committed to communicating with someone with BPD. I am hopeful this material will provide you with a framework to maintain and improve your relationship with the one you care about.

How This Book Can Help You

Preserving a caring relationship with someone with BPD can be arduous. You love this person, yet you feel he is constantly resisting and challenging your caring. In these pages you will recognize some of the common dilemmas you encounter in loving someone with BPD. You will recognize the portrayals of the struggles that emerge.

This book was written for you, the communicating partner. It will help you recognize when a crisis may be developing in your dealings with your loved one. You will learn specific strategies to help you adapt to common frustrations in the relationship. These methods are relatively easy to keep in mind and apply. I present multiple examples of how you can utilize these strategies in working toward a healthier relationship.

One of the primary approaches I describe is called SET-UP: support, empathy, truth–understanding, perseverance. This simple acronym represents a way of thinking when interacting with your loved one. The SET component is the main focus for the communication system, as support, empathy, and truth should be balanced elements in each communication and should be emphasized in each verbal interaction. Understanding and perseverance are more general, overarching attitudes and thus comprise the supplementary component.

I developed the primary SET system of communication for clinicians and for those in the general public who engage with challenging people. It is designed to help maintain a mind-set that can minimize escalation of tension. SET communication is easily and quickly learned. It is easy to remember and implement. Keeping the SET segment prominently in mind during communications also helps you recognize when your interventions are not being "heard" by your loved one and how you can therefore adapt your approach. UP is a goal throughout the relationship— maintaining an ongoing perspective of understanding and perseverance.

SET-UP is not a way to cure a borderline individual but, rather, a technique to help you, the individual's communication partner, relate to her. It is not a treatment protocol, although it can be immersed in a therapy program. In addition to discussing specific ways to institute SET-UP, this book presents other interaction strategies as well, along with ways to recognize when they can be constructively introduced. The ultimate goal in employing these approaches is to establish ongoing, respectful interactions that preserve the relationship with your loved one.

What's Inside This Book

The first part of this book presents necessary general information: Chapter 1 reviews our current understanding of BPD and the kinds of communication problems inherent in the disorder; chapter 2 reviews what SET-UP is (and is not) and how it can be used most effectively; and chapter 3 describes other, supplementary techniques that can be helpful in interactions with those with BPD.

The second part of the book addresses specific challenges that emerge during these exchanges. This section presents multiple dilemmas often encountered, scenarios frequently observed, and ways to deal with these conflicts. A final chapter examines when you need to consider if the relationship can endure.

This book expands on the SET-UP construct and, I hope, will help ease the distress experienced by those with BPD and those who love them.

About the Author

My interest in BPD extends back forty years, to the time of my psychiatric training, initially in medical school at Cornell University in New York, and later during my residency at the National Institute of Mental Health in Washington, DC. I began seeing more patients who fulfilled characteristics that were just beginning to be documented with a formal diagnosis of borderline personality disorder. Some of my colleagues disliked dealing with them, but I found many of these individuals to be intriguing, motivated, and courageous. Their anger and pain cried out from a history of hurt and disappointment.

My interest has led me to the publication of many articles and two books on BPD. For the past thirty-five years I have had the opportunity to lecture to professional and lay audiences in the United States and abroad. What has engendered the most interest during these interactions is discussion of the SET system of communication, first developed in a hospital program in St. Louis. SET is described in my first book with Hal Straus, *I Hate You—Don't Leave Me*, and extended in our second, *Sometimes I Act Crazy*. Most questions and discussions have centered on requests for more examples of how SET can be utilized as a coherent model of thought while communicating with others, especially the often fraught interactions with borderline individuals. This work is an attempt to respond to these requests.

Note to the Reader

As explained in my two other books, I have taken the liberty of invoking several shorthand references to simplify the writing in this work. Although I abhor the use of a label to refer to a human being (as in, "The diabetic is in exam room three"), I sometimes apply the concise designation "BP" to represent the more appropriate but lengthy phrase "a human being who exhibits symptoms descriptive of a psychiatric diagnosis of borderline personality disorder."

Likewise, for lack of a better all-encompassing identifier, I sometimes use the unsatisfactory term "partner" to refer to you, the reader—the significant other, family member, or loved one who consistently interacts with an individual with BPD.

Also, rather than using the awkward "he/she" or "him/her" throughout the book, I simply alternate pronouns, trusting you will grant me this liberty to streamline the text.

Lastly and most significantly, I wish to emphasize that the "P" in BP and BPD represents an actual, real, feeling person. It is in the spirit of deep respect for you and the person you love that I offer this work.

PART
ONE

COPING
TOOLS
FOR BPD

CHAPTER 1

An Overview of Borderline Personality

Borderline personality disorder is an illness that can torment not only those who carry the diagnosis, but also others who interact with them. If you're reading this book, you are likely already acquainted with the diagnosis. You have read about it. You have seen it portrayed (usually negatively) on television and in books, plays, movies, and music. You also care about someone who fits the diagnostic criteria. But BPD is more than a label. It defines individuals who may be experiencing tremendous internal pain, which may radiate into the marrow of those who are close to them—individuals like Jamie.

> Jamie's life was a collage of fragments. By day she was a caring, friendly nurse. At night she felt friendless and self-condemning. She could feign contentment, but she felt mostly sadness. Her anger pushed people away, yet she craved protection and felt abandoned. She yearned for others to fill in the gaps, to caulk the roughened edges. When she lacked self-esteem, they would be confident. When she was emotional, they would be calm. When she couldn't comprehend her feelings, they would understand

her. But she felt that none of the others in her life could fulfill these needs.

The purpose of this book is to help you better understand this disorder and to propose communication techniques that will help sustain a sturdy relationship with someone with BPD. In a healthy relationship you can learn how to love and stay with someone with BPD, without losing yourself.

This chapter describes the defining factors and various ways you may experience borderline symptoms in a loved one. You will recognize common characteristics that illustrate BPD. You may be frustrated, confused, and angered by this behavior. Recognizing and understanding the various presentations of BPD is a first step in preparing constructive methods of interaction.

Perceptions of BPD

Our understanding of borderline personality disorder has evolved over many years. How we define it, treat it, and identify how people survive its infliction have changed greatly. Centuries ago physicians identified individuals who displayed severe ranges of emotion: they loved to great heights the same people they reviled beyond depths; they were impulsive and self-destructive. Some thought they were possessed by demons and required religious exorcism instead of medical ministrations. In the twentieth century such an individual was identified as the "Hateful Patient," who demanded everything from doctors but defied all tending.

Eighty years ago such patients were first called "borderline," signifying a level of function on the border between the prevailing concepts of *psychosis* (a complete break with reality) and *neurosis* (syndromes of anxiety and situational depression). Later identification placed the diagnosis in the realm of schizophrenia. Today we conceptualize BPD as a personality style with specific, identifying symptoms, distinguishable from other diagnoses.

For many years such patients were thought to be untreatable, as well as unbearable. Doctors felt these individuals did not respond to any therapy regimen and never got better. But more recent studies confirm a much more favorable prognosis. The McLean Study of Adult Development and the Collaborative Longitudinal Personality Disorders Study (at Harvard University, sponsored by the National Institute of Mental Health) have been assessing BPD patients since 2000. The resultant reports demonstrate that most patients get better over time, some even without formal treatment. Several therapy models have been developed specifically to treat BPD. Dialectical behavior therapy, mentalization-based therapy, transference-focused psychotherapy, and others employ treatment protocols that address individual borderline symptoms.

Defining BPD

The *Diagnostic and Statistical Manual of Mental Disorders, Fifth Edition* (DSM-5), published in 2013, contains the current, universally accepted definition of borderline personality disorder. This definition has changed only slightly from what appeared in the third edition of DSM, published in 1980, and relies on descriptive symptoms. This *categorical* designation lists nine defining criteria, five or more of which must be documented in order to establish a BPD diagnosis:

1. Frantic efforts to avoid real or imagined abandonment

2. Unstable and intense interpersonal relationships alternating between extremes of idealization and devaluation

3. Lack of clear and consistent sense of identity and self-image

4. Impulsiveness in potentially self-damaging behaviors, such as drug abuse, spending, sex, binge eating, reckless driving

5. Recurrent suicidal behavior, gestures, or threats, or self-mutilating behavior

6. Severe mood changes and extreme reactivity to situational stresses

7. Chronic feelings of emptiness

8. Frequent, inappropriate, uncontrollable episodes of anger

9. Transient, stress-related feelings of unreality or paranoia

(An alternative to this structured model of definition appears in the appendix of DSM-5. This paradigm endorses a *dimensional* model of BPD, in which behaviors are evaluated on a spectrum of severity, in a sense measuring degrees of "borderlineishness" and to what extent symptoms interfere with functioning. Both models emphasize the primary mechanisms that are emblematic of the disorder: mood and emotional instability; impulsivity and dangerous, uncontrolled behavior; instability of relationships; unpredictable anger outbursts; and identity confusion.)

Splitting

BPD is characterized by a number of *defense mechanisms,* or basic emotional reactions. The primary, animating defense mechanism of BPD is *splitting,* the need to divide contradictory perceptions. It is the inability to simultaneously hold both positive and negative experiences about a person or situation. In this way the BP avoids the contradictions and ambiguities encountered in life. But for the person in partnership with the BP, splitting can be the most challenging feature of the disorder.

Splitting does not allow the BP to see any fault in a loved one, nor any goodness in an antagonist. This black-or-white thinking results in idealization or devaluation of people and positions. It is as if the BP sees two separate people: the "good you" and the "bad you." The good you is idolized. Any negative features are either ignored or projected onto others, or onto the bad you. Conversely, the bad you has no redeeming qualities and can be hated without reservation. These pure perceptions lack consistency and may change dramatically. Other primitive mechanisms evolve, which may result in superstitions, compulsions, phobias, and other magical thinking. As we will see in later chapters, splitting affects many characteristics of BPD.

BPD Passions and Dangerous Relationships

The constellation of symptoms that we label BPD has profound effects on the person experiencing it, and it may be disturbing and mystifying to you as well. The BP is a thesaurus of reactions. When one attitude or behavior doesn't fit the situation, he dials up and substitutes another. He may yearn for someone to care for him, then rage and rebel when his dependency translates into feeling imprisoned. He is unable to trust himself to make simple decisions. He may meld agreeably into any political group, yet when alone, he may not apprehend what he really believes. He may feel unable to control self-harming behaviors, then be mystified by the sense of calm and lack of pain he perceives when blood trickles from a self-administered wound. Extreme emotions spill everywhere. Prick a passion, stab a sentiment, mash an emotion, and the BP bleeds out his sensitivities like an emotional hemophiliac.

Borderline symptoms including poor self-image, unstable sense of identity, emotional instability, and impulsivity make the BP vulnerable to attachment to individuals with complementary features. She is often attracted to people who exhibit self-assurance and strength. A sense of confidence and power can be very appealing to the BP, who longs to be taken care of by a powerful partner she hopes will protect her and direct her to a better life.

This is why the BP's disappointing romantic history may include relationships with individuals displaying narcissistic personality disorder (NPD), whose self-confidence is only a mask to conceal underlying insecurities. The narcissist projects an aura of impenetrable self-confidence and entitlement. He is preoccupied with maintaining an image of power and success and requires constant admiration. He may exaggerate his accomplishments and yearn for the perfect job and the perfect mate. However, the individual with pathological NPD lacks empathy and the ability to genuinely understand another's feelings. Inevitably, the BP's relationship with a pathological narcissist crashes. In contrast, a confident, healthy partner, like you, who develops the ability to communicate empathically, can make the relationship work.

How BPD Affects Others

For the loved ones of individuals with BPD, borderline behavior can be confounding. The BP craves relationships, yet constantly challenges those with whom he is in relationships. His sudden rage may erupt from the smallest provocation, blocking attempts at closeness. The BP's fear of abandonment battles his fears of engulfment and distrust of closeness. Feelings of emptiness hinder intimacy. And the need for another to fill that emptiness may be all-consuming.

When you exhibit a flaw, you suddenly mutate into a despised villain. There is no gray area, no compromise—all is perfect or all is hopeless. Arguing is useless, as you end up repeating the same logic to someone who doesn't comprehend it. It can be like shouting into an echoing abyss where there is rebounded a circling, obscure response, or a tangential response, or no response at all. You feel manipulated, and you may even begin to doubt your own perceptions.

Many of the defining features of the BPD syndrome are painful, primarily *internalized* experiences. Abandonment fears, insecurities about relationships, feelings of emptiness, and a blurred sense of identity may be hidden from others. The BP may experience brief feelings of unreality or paranoia that are frightening and that she may fear to share. She also may conceal her reactive mood vacillations, black-white reactivity, and rejection sensitivity. But her partner will more likely experience the outwardly expressed, *externalized* behaviors. These include rage reactions, suspicious distrust, impulsive and reckless self-damaging behaviors, and suicidal gestures. The following chapters describe ways to respond to your loved one's periodic challenges. But know that over time, with UP (understanding and perseverance), your relationship can survive and flourish.

Addressing the Diagnosis

Now that BPD is more commonly referenced, many cling to or debate the existence of the diagnosis. Some who are endowed with the BPD label invoke it as an explanation of their behavior: "It's just my BPD." "My borderline personality made me do it." Others disavow the diagnosis that may have been bestowed on them by a professional or nonprofessional; I frequently hear the disparaging complaint "My ex was a borderline."

Some partners get caught up in debating the issue. But it is important to understand that psychiatric diagnoses, and many other medical diagnoses, are defined exclusively by overt symptoms. Understanding and differentiating these disorders on a microscopic level is not yet available. In this sense psychiatric diagnoses are comparable to where we stood with most medical diagnoses in the last century. In years past a doctor could diagnose pneumonia based on signs of fever, wheezing, and cough, but could not discern if the etiology was bacterial, viral, fungal, or carcinogenic. Although great strides continue to be made in understanding genetic, biological, and physiological underpinnings of psychopathology, psychiatric diagnoses are still based primarily on observable and reported symptoms.

Debating with your loved one over which one of you is borderline is fruitless. More important than gaining consensus regarding a particular medical diagnosis is agreeing on what situations are pathological to the relationship and deciding to address specific, troublesome behaviors. Improving the relationship you have with your loved one is much more important than assigning a diagnostic label.

BPD and Other Diagnoses

BPD is typically *associated* with other disorders in several ways. BPD may coexist with other illnesses, most commonly depression and anxiety. Phobias, obsessive-compulsive disorder, and social anxiety disorder may be accompanying diagnoses. Impulsivity and severe frustration may be signs of coinciding attention deficit disorder.

BPD may be discounted or *confused* with another diagnosis. An initial call for help that describes sadness over a failed relationship or intoxication after disappointment may mislead. This may cause others to overlook the BPD diagnosis and instead focus only on depressive symptoms or substance use. Depictions of severe mood swings may mistakenly suggest bipolar disorder, which is statistically less prevalent than BPD. (BPD mood changes tend to change more dramatically, more often responding to situational stimuli. Also, BPD emotional swings generally extend for hours, rather than days or weeks, as in bipolar disorder.) Manipulation and excessive rage may imply antisocial or narcissistic personality disorder. Transient paranoid feelings may mimic schizophrenia.

BPD may *camouflage* and cover other symptoms. Extreme behavioral changes may mask underlying substance abuse or an eating disorder, which may not be recognized. Other addictive disorders, such as gambling or pornography compulsions, may be diluted in the flooding deluge of borderline symptoms.

You may observe other serious symptoms peeking out around a BPD diagnosis. You and your loved one should acknowledge these problems. Seeking help is important. And it is especially important that the BP is openly relating these difficulties to the clinician. If agreeable, you may on occasion want to accompany the BP to visits with the doctor and therapist.

Origins of BPD

Nature-versus-nurture arguments about what causes BPD have been refined, because experts agree that both contribute. DSM-5 notes that BPD is often diagnosed within families. But this genetic predisposition does not necessarily decree the development of BPD in other family members. The illness is often (but not always) associated with trauma during childhood development, especially physical, emotional, and sexual abuse. Much ongoing research in BPD continues to examine the mutual interactions among environment and biology and genetics.

Let's take a closer look at Jamie now, to see how these interactions present themselves in her life:

Twenty-nine-year old Jamie was a nurse working on a hospital psychiatric unit. To the patients, she appeared insightful and empathetic. The staff experienced her to be secure and supportive, sometimes too supportive—her hugs seemed a little too tight and seemed to last a little too long. Her displays of affection for others compensated for her inability to soothe herself. And her empathy for others' suffering reflected a scrupulous identification with emotional pain.

Through adolescence and beyond, Jamie preferred the company of men. She favored sports and "serious" conversation, like men. Girls, to her mind, were gossipy, competitive, and uninteresting. Attachments didn't last long, but there was always the need for a boyfriend. When a relationship seemed foundering, she began prospecting for the next, sometimes resorting to settling for a previous one.

Some boyfriends were angry and demanding. Jamie knew those contacts would eventually terminate, and she could wait for an appropriate time. But some men were caring and understanding, trying their best to make her happy. Those relationships frightened Jamie. She intuited that she would ultimately drive them away, and so she was always anxiously awaiting that shoe to drop. As they satisfied one demand, she would immediately propose more hurdles. There was a need to push them away, for the anticipation of that dropping shoe was too much. She had a sense that she needed to "hurry up and get it over with already."

For a while she settled for Rod, the handyman at a nearby apartment building. Rod drank a lot, was unreliable, and was often unfaithful. But occasional sex with him was acceptable if unexceptional, and Rod made few demands.

At a hospital Christmas party Jamie was flattered by the attention of Jack, a board member of the hospital, twenty years her senior. Jack charmed and teased her while complaining about the horrors he was enduring in his second divorce. They began dating. Jack took Jamie to expensive restaurants, concerts, and sporting events. Jamie saw Jack as someone who was strong and would take care of her. Jack saw Jamie as an attractive accessory who admired him and would be mentored by his worldliness. A narcissist and a borderline—a "perfect storm" match.

Eventually, Jack's suggestions felt like demands, and his directions seemed controlling. For Jack, Jamie's early deferrals and compliance mutated into petulant rebelliousness and sudden fits of fury. For Jamie, a satisfying, healthy relationship could develop not with someone who tried to control her, nor with someone who remained superficial. So this "perfect" relationship, too, ended.

An enduring partner for Jamie would be someone who understood her struggles, persevered through the obstacles she constructed, and maintained caring, consistent communication.

You know someone like Jamie. She may be your wife, your partner, your daughter, your mother, your good friend. Change a few gender characteristics and he could be your partner, your son, your father.

Jamie's path reflects many features and challenges in connecting with a loved one with BPD. You may recognize the kinds of behavior the BP often exhibits. The one you care about can display sometimes puzzling twists and turns in her reactions to you and others.

Though she may push you away, she wants you to stay. And if you do stay, adjusting your ways of interacting may be necessary. If you can ride out the storm long enough, she will continue to be a person you want to keep in your life. But as you maintain the relationship, there are some things to know about borderline personality—for her sake, and yours.

Some Truths About BPD

It is truly a profound display of caring commitment to maintain your love for someone struggling with BPD. You may be challenged multiple times. But here you are, reading a book that you hope will help you better cope with this relationship. Your love and support are admirable in trying to improve your communication skills with this special person. Hopefully, your dedication will be enhanced with the skills described in this book.

As you continue the relationship, these facts about BPD may help you balance enduring obstacles with the reward of maintaining a loving bond:

- Although BPs can be confusing, disruptive, and maddening, many are creative, intelligent, sensitive, and successful.

- Although there may be recurrences of some symptoms, most BPs get better with treatment. Indeed, the DSM-5 summary of the disorder notes that over time many progress to a point at which the level of function no longer supports a formal diagnosis of BPD.

- Many BPs refuse to get help or terminate therapy prematurely. But the long-term research cited in DSM-5 (and many other outcome studies) demonstrates that many of those individuals also get better. It just might take longer. In particular, intense mood changes, suicidal gestures, rage episodes, and extreme impulsivity usually subside over time.

- Maintaining your own health with appropriate protections for yourself is best for all involved.

Learning to be with someone with BPD can be a consuming challenge. The rest of this book is dedicated to trying to help you with that challenge. This book will teach you effective communication skills that help you stay at your loved one's side. The next two chapters describe techniques to more effectively deal with aspects of BPD.

CHAPTER 2

The SET-UP
Communication Style

Interactions with individuals with borderline personality disorder are turbulent for many reasons. Feeling alone, restless, misunderstood, helpless, and out of control, the BP may exhibit unpredictable rage, self-destructiveness, impulsivity, and wildly contradictory moods. Rubbing against the edges of someone with BPD can be like rubbing the corners of a corrugated box. Push too hard on the textured furrows and they turn into a serrated blade that can draw blood. Perceiving the world in black-or-white terms, envisioning a climate that undulates from wonderful to terrible, and evaluating people the same way—all this complicates personal connections. Caring for a BP can be hard work! You may be constantly tested, your commitment always questioned. Learning what to say and what not to say is difficult. Often, nothing you say is satisfying. Even well-trained professionals accept that treating BPD can be frustrating and challenging.

This chapter introduces the SET-UP method of communication. I designed this approach to outline a practical way to interact with borderline individuals. SET-UP describes ways for you to anticipate and respond to conflicts in the moment. It also focuses on borderline responses that signal areas that you should emphasize during the interaction.

What Is SET-UP?

SET-UP was initially developed in the early 1980s from a hospital-based program designed for borderline patients. It is a communication system first taught to hospital staff, then to loved ones of patients. Although aimed specifically at dealing with borderline individuals, you can use SET-UP for interactions with others, especially adolescents, during stressful situations. It is a simple, structured framework, easily taught and retained, to base communication with a BP.

SET—an acronym for "support, empathy, and truth"—is a practical approach to interactions with a BP. UP represents "understanding and perseverance," the goals that the BP and the BP's partner attempt to achieve in the relationship. The SET portion is a straightforward conversation-guided technique. It is utilized in every interaction with the BP. The UP segment supplements ongoing SET communication. UP focuses on maintaining a general acceptance of your loved one and denotes an overall attitude to maintain in the relationship.

SET expression is not a formalized treatment. Unlike standard therapy programs designed for long-term behavioral changes, SET was developed to address acute, day-to-day situations and to avoid escalation during potential conflicts. Nevertheless, the goals of SET, utilized by loved ones, are consistent with those of formal programs conducted by professionals:

- Like cognitive behavioral therapy, SET attempts to create a setting that helps the BP recognize unproductive behavior and alter it.

- Like dialectical behavior therapy, SET focuses on improvement in mood and control of destructive impulses.

- Like mentalization-based therapy, SET emphasizes empathy and confronts problems of trust and relationships.

- Like schema-focused therapy, SET deals with rejection hypersensitivity and abandonment concerns.

- Like exposure therapy for post-traumatic stress disorder and phobias, SET confronts feared situations.

- Like these and other formal programs, SET encourages a combination of mindfulness/mentalization and the courage to confront painful reality dilemmas.

Support, Empathy, Truth: The SET Mind-Set

SET is a three-part system of dialogue (see figure 2–1).

The S (support) component is an "I" statement of concern and commitment. Support emphasizes your personal concern and desire to help. S statements include: "I am concerned about how you are feeling"; "I am worried about what is happening to you"; "I want to try to help."

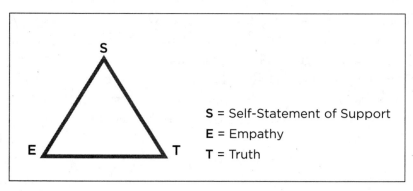

S = Self-Statement of Support
E = Empathy
T = Truth

Figure 2–1

The E portion communicates empathy and is a "you" recognition. It acknowledges the anguish and conflicted feelings of the BP. Empathy should emphasize the BP's experience, not yours. E statements might be: "This must be a terrible time for you"; "You must be feeling really desperate to resort to this"; "No one can imagine how painful this must be for you."

T (truth) focuses on a realistic estimation of the situation and the BP's primary responsibility in addressing these issues. Truth emphasizes that while others can contribute, the BP must be aware of his participation in predictable consequences. Support and empathy statements are subjective declarations. They recognize the feelings of all involved. Truth statements address the practical options of what can be done to deal with current problems. Truth is best expressed in accepting, but neutral, matter-of-fact ways: "We know what happened... We have to deal with the consequences... Here are some ways I can help... Now what are you going to do?" The T point of the SET triangle is the most challenging for the BP, because it confronts the BP's attempts to avoid the situation and demands practical problem solving. Individual responsibility is emphasized, without blaming or wallowing in feelings of helplessness.

The UP addition to the SET framework is an ongoing reminder to both you and your loved one that healthy interactions require understanding and perseverance throughout the relationship. Understanding of borderline pathology is essential for all parties to grasp. But understanding does not absolve anyone of responsibility for behavior. Perseverance is a reminder that the commitment to each other must survive disappointments and frustrations. Sometimes the best way to handle difficult interactions is to just hang in there.

Using SET

Ideally, each interaction with the BP balances all three elements of the SET triad in relatively equal proportions. Following a conflict, a destructive behavior, or some other situation in which dialogue may be strained, SET can be useful:

"I am very concerned about what has happened and want to help" (SUPPORT).

"You must have been really upset to do that" (EMPATHY).

"We need to figure out what to do about this now" (TRUTH).

If, however, one side of the interaction is not expressed, or if the BP does not absorb one expression, you will encounter predictable responses. When you hear a particular defensive retort, it should draw attention to that portion of SET that is not being "heard." Special attention should be focused on that side, and you should attempt to reinforce the incomplete communication.

When the support piece is not absorbed, the BP will accuse you of not caring or not wanting to help (see figure 2–2). Any kind of "you don't care about me" rejoinder signifies that support needs to be reemphasized. You may then get reeled into conflict:
"You really don't want to help me."
"Yes, I do."
"No, you don't."
"Yes, I do."
And on and on.

You may not realize you have been pulled into this unproductive interaction until you are buried in it. At such a point it is important to recognize your own frustration and change directions. Recognizing the BP's inability to accept support suggests the need to reinforce it: "It must be hard to accept that anyone really cares about you after all you've been through, but I really do want to try to help."

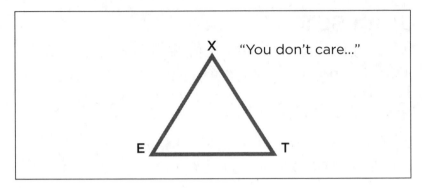

Figure 2–2

When the empathy portion of the triangle is not expressed or accepted, the BP's predictable response is an angry accusation that she is not being understood: "You just can't understand how I feel" (see figure 2–3). Here again, you want to avoid a back-and-forth discourse, attempting to insist on your caring, or being manipulated into taking over responsibility. It may be helpful to focus on your awareness of the unique anguish the BP is experiencing: "It's hard to imagine how much pain you must be enduring." "You must be feeling horrible to go through all this." "Maybe you feel that no one can understand what this is like."

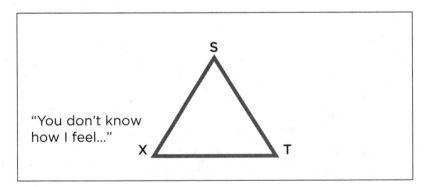

Figure 2–3

A more complex dilemma emerges when the truth portion is not clearly conveyed. Both you and the BP may collude in avoiding facing reality issues. But avoidance of real-world predicaments reinforces the BP's denial that he has responsibility for stressful interactions or that any problems even exist. Avoidance-of-truth interactions may temporarily dodge conflict. Indeed, the situation may tranquilize, and the BP's underlying defensive anger may be subdued for a while. But this·joint avoidance of reality cannot last.

Although it is tempting to evade challenging the BP, you may be inadvertently encouraging unrealistic expectations in an enmeshment of denial (see figure 2–4). Eventually, real-world issues that only the BP can deal with will puncture the short-term placidity. Ultimately, the BP's anticipation of magical resolutions of problems is frustrated, and her disappointment and anger will be ignited. The longer truth is avoided, the more extreme the ultimate conflagration will be. At some point you will need to inject reality assessments: "We need to take a look at this problem and decide how to deal with it."

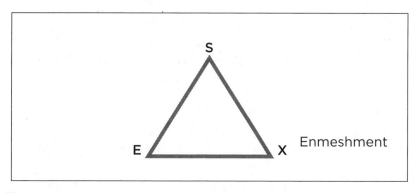

Figure 2–4

What SET Is Not

Support is *not* identification with the BP. "Yeah, that happened to me, too" is not a helpful S declaration and will be dismissed as irrelevant. "I" statements proclaim your own concern and commitment to help.

Empathy is *not* sympathy. "I feel so sorry for you" is condescending and does not express acceptance of the BP's pain. "I know just how you feel" will often be countered by an angry (and deserved) response asserting the reality that no one truly feels what the BP is experiencing. An E statement is a "you" declaration that acknowledges the BP's experience, not yours.

Truth is *not* hard-ass confrontation. Truth without support or empathy is a perversion of "tough love." Truth does not invalidate the BP's experience. Statements such as "You're overreacting," "It wasn't that bad," "That's not what happened," and "I never said that" invite arguments that won't be resolved and are distractions from dealing with the necessary responses to the ensuing dilemmas. Truth also does not fixate on blame or second-guessing recrimination: "This is all your fault." "This is a fine mess you got us into." "You made your bed, now lie in it." "This wouldn't have happened if you would have just…" T statements should emphasize neutral problem solving, not disparaging reprimand, which only results in more defensiveness and avoidance of self-review.

Gordon was upset when the bank called to inform him that his twenty-three-year-old daughter Janet's account was again overdrawn by almost a thousand dollars. He was frustrated and angry, but he prepared to discuss this recurring problem with her. First, he took time to cool off. Gordon knew that if his anger exploded, it would only inflame the situation and result in Janet's defensiveness leading her to focus on his anger rather than on the financial concern. He rehearsed SET statements in his mind and how he would present this concern to her. He waited until after dinner to start the conversation, when both of them were relaxed.

Gordon: "Janet, the bank called me today and told me you are way overdrawn. I thought there was plenty in your account. I'm concerned about what happened."

Janet: "I had to buy a few things. So what? I can't run and tell you everything I do. Don't be so obsessive! The bank will cover me."

Gordon: [feeling himself getting angry at her defensiveness and dismissive attitude, but working to hold in his frustration] "Well, I'm curious about what you bought. I just want to make sure you are handling your finances."

Janet: [feeling defensive] "I don't need your help! You know that shopping makes me feel better. I decided I needed to freshen my wardrobe. And I splurged with an expensive purse. Big deal!"

Gordon: "I understand that sometimes when you're feeling down, you go shopping. I'm disturbed that maybe you're not feeling well. Can I help?" (SUPPORT).

Janet: "It's just that school and work have been a strain. It's been a long, gloomy winter, and sometimes I just need to cheer myself up."

Gordon: "It sounds like you've been having a hard time lately" (EMPATHY).

Janet: [not hearing the support messages] "Well, that's what I'm saying! Can't you understand? I really don't give a shit about your little budget!"

Gordon: "I just want to help when you're stressed (SUPPORT). And, you know, the bank has given you a hard time before. They could complicate your student loans. A bad credit rating could jeopardize future financial needs (TRUTH). I know how important it is for you to be recognized as responsible. Look how hard you've been working with the job and keeping your grades up (EMPATHY). I just want you to know that I love you and want to help you be the smart, accomplished, and wonderful woman you are. If you're not feeling well or there's any problem, you know you can come to me and we'll work it out together (SUPPORT). Let's talk about how you want to handle the overdraft and how you can protect yourself in the future" (TRUTH).

It can be a monumental challenge to control your own feelings while trying to balance equally the SET triad. You may sometimes fail to maintain composure in the face of accusations or destructive behaviors. But if you can simultaneously continue to express support, acknowledge empathy, yet present truth, you can successfully defuse many crises. Adding the UP portion of the communication approach will keep you focused on the attitudes you want to maintain during troublesome interactions. Understanding and perseverance are necessary characteristics for the partner who cares for the BP and hopes to work with her in establishing a healthier relationship.

Action Steps

Think SET.

Keep in mind SET phrases and be aware when the BP reflects evidence that one side of the triangle is lacking:

"I love you and really want to help you get through this."

"*You* must be going through a really tough time."

"How can we work together to make it better? Here's what I can do. What do you think you need to do?"

Understand and persevere.

As we considered in chapter 1, there is little Technicolor in the cinematic world of BPD. Situations are black or white, good or bad. People are heroes or villains. This concept of "splitting" is the primary defense mechanism of BPD. It is a vestige of childhood, which abhors ambivalence and ambiguity. Most mature adults accept the uncertainties of existence. Friends, clubs, jobs, political affiliations—all have flaws, which must be accepted and compromised. But after a minor misunderstanding the BP might transform his lover into a hated demon. Or after a conflict he might reinforce his own self-image as a powerless, blameless victim.

It is important for you to recognize the whipsaw expressions of splitting. This is where the "understanding" and "perseverance" of SET-UP come in. When you are projected as the villain, *it ain't personal!* Accept that it is a reflection of the BP's confusion over her ambivalence. She wrestles with accepting that you (and the rest of the world) have both good and bad qualities and that relationships can be maintained without insisting that people must be only good or only bad. These conflicts may also be directed at the BP herself, when she projects all wrong on herself. UP helps you hang in there when the relationship becomes challenging. Even if the intimacy can't be maintained, you can employ UP, if you choose, to continue the connection on a different level. Sometimes, though, you may indeed decide to "just be friends."

Rita and Patty had been friends since high school. Their spouses were friends, and their kids played together. But

Patty would be mystified when Rita would occasionally withdraw, not return phone calls, and seem annoyed when contacted. Then, after a while, things would return to normal, and Rita would act as if nothing had happened. When Patty asked Rita about her distancing, Rita would deny any problems, just saying she was busy with her family and her work as a real estate agent.

When Patty and her husband decided to buy a house, they agreed it would be better not to engage Rita or any friend to help with this project. Soon after they bought a house, Patty received a furious call from Rita, chastising Patty for not using her as their agent. Surprised at the intensity of Rita's outrage, Patty explained that she didn't want to involve her or any friend in this big decision that could threaten a relationship. Patty then added that she never intended to upset Rita and apologized for disappointing her. Shockingly, Rita then declared that she would no longer be Patty's friend; she canceled their weekend plans together and shrieked she would no longer talk to her.

Patty was stunned. Looking back on their relationship, she now understood this pattern in Rita's behavior. Patty recognized that what she had considered a close friendship had always been tainted by Rita's tantrums. Patty decided that she should either completely withdraw from the friendship or accept a different kind of relationship that accommodated Rita's erratic sensibilities. She decided that she didn't want to completely discard the affiliation between the families, but she had to accept that she could not maintain a closer connection. Instead, she would persevere and relate to Rita on a muted level. She called Rita to invite her kids for a playdate. She was friendly at social occasions. From then on, Patty preserved a more superficial, but acceptable association with Rita.

Anticipate.

Rehearse how you might approach the BP. Think of how you want to deal with the problem and how you might phrase your communication. Especially, think through how you can present SET statements.

> Your adult son quit his latest job after again complaining about the unfairness of his boss and arguing with him. He comes to you, justifying his exit and wondering what he should do now:
>
> "It really must have been hard for you to deal with that situation" (EMPATHY).
>
> "I'm glad you came to me, because I would like to help" (SUPPORT).
>
> "We need to look at this pattern, because this has happened a few times now. How can we work at learning to tolerate issues like this when they emerge with difficult bosses and coworkers? I know you want to work, and you may need to put up with some of these difficulties. Let's talk some more about what has been happening with these jobs and look at ways to deal with them" (TRUTH).

Emphasize the positive.

Focus on strengths. Reinforce achievements attained despite barriers:

"I'm really proud of you for confronting this difficult situation" (SUPPORT).

"Of course, it hasn't been easy for you" (EMPATHY).

"Obviously, though, there are still things to work out. What else do we need to do?" (TRUTH).

Monitor your reactions—try to stay calm and neutral.

Omit criticism in your support and empathy statements. Don't tie these with "but/if" phrases, such as "I want to support you, if you can stop being so difficult" or "You're suffering through a difficult time, but you're just making it worse." Confrontation regarding responsibility is contained in separate truth statements, which should be delivered in a nonjudgmental, practical manner, preferably after priming with support and empathy. Sometimes presenting a truth statement as a question to the BP is less threatening, and it evokes a reminder that she has responsibility:

"How do you think we should handle this?"

"What's your next step for dealing with this problem?"

Keep truth statements primarily in the present, not the past.

The BP may evade the truth by referring to past wounds or others' experiences: "The boss keeps hurting my feelings." "I tried that before…it never works." "James got in trouble for that."

Don't get distracted by talking about what happened before. Truth is best expressed as "What are you going to about it *now*?"

Keeping the SET dialogue and the UP frame of reference in mind is a useful model in which to manage interactions. It is designed not only to shape the conversation, but also to address responses that may require reinforcing statements. The ultimate goal of SET-UP is to maintain communication and avoid derailing the interaction.

The next chapter describes complementary techniques that fit within a SET-UP approach.

CHAPTER 3

Complementary Techniques

SET-UP principles can be embedded in other techniques to cope with BPD interactions. Some of these approaches are part of a SET-UP method, while others complement SET-UP. This chapter describes other methods to deal with borderline challenges.

Provide Transitional Objects

Personal support communication is usually transmitted through direct talk, but it can also be conveyed through material representation. A child's "blankie" or doll to which he tenaciously clings, for example, is accepted as a representation of the mothering figure when she is not present. Child psychiatrists understand this behavior as reflecting the child's transition from his primitive demand for the parent's constant, protective presence to acceptance of the parent's existence when out of sight. Eventually, the healthy child achieves what is termed *object constancy*, which is the realization that the parental figure continues to exist when out of the child's immediate presence.

The normal development of object constancy, which in turn leads to the development of trusting behavior, usually requires reliable, nurturing parenting in the early years. But the BP is often deprived of this progression—the result of an unstable childhood. Thus, she does not experience consistent behaviors from others. This lack of dependability impairs development of trust. Like an infant who cries in fear when her mother leaves the room, the BP is vulnerable to feelings of abandonment. Also, like an infant, immediate feelings define an attitude. The snapshot emotion of what the BP feels *right now* determines her judgment. A hungry infant is angry at the parent, but then adores her when fed. Likewise, acute reactions to a current situation define the BP's shifting black-white reactions.

A transitional object given to the BP can calm fears of abandonment and may temper angry swings toward the partner who leaves. A smiling picture given to a loved one represents you when you are gone and revives pleasant memories. Other possessions accomplish the same thing, as in these instances:

- When Brad's partner, Steven, was away on frequent business trips, Brad would sleep with Steven's sweatshirt. This familiar object and scent relaxed him at night and allayed his frustration at Steven's frequent absences.

- When Evelyn moved into a dorm across town from her mother for her freshman year of college, she kept in her purse a picture of them together, which she frequently consulted when lonely.

Make Predictions

A useful approach can be verbally walking the BP through the likely outcome of threatened behavior. After establishing support and empathy groundwork, predicting likely truth consequences is helpful in a variety of ways. First, it encourages the BP to better evaluate impulsive behavior and think through the probable consequences of his actions. Second, it is reassuring to the BP that you can understand and anticipate what to him may seem to be uncontrollable and unpredictable behavior. It can also stimulate *oppositionality*—the intentional resistance to conform to expectations—such that the BP actually reacts more constructively: "So, you think I'm just going to start yelling and run off. I'll show you. I'm just going to sit here quietly and not say a word— just to piss you off!"

Predicting should not be presented in an accusatory, angry manner: "Oh, there you go again!" Instead, present it in a relaxed, matter-of-fact way. You are not reprimanding. You are merely presenting the likely results of the BP's actions.

> Fifteen-year-old Jenny, after a conflict with her father, called to tell him she and her older boyfriend, Tyler, were running off together.
>
> "Jen, I hate for you to be so upset. Please come home and let's see if we can talk this out."
>
> "I'm never coming home. You put me in the hospital before, just because Tyler and I were partying. And you're always trying to control where I go and who I'm with and when I should come home. I'm not a child, and I can do what I want and be with who I want to be with."
>
> "Yes, Jen. You are growing up, but you're still a minor, saying you're running away. So that means, legally, I have to call the police. And you know they'll have to pick you up. And then they'll probably take you back to the hospital. And I know how much you hate being there. But this time they would probably keep you longer. And then Tyler will probably get in trouble too. I really don't want us to go through all this. Why not just come home first. And then we can talk some more about it."

Explicitly describing the likely results of the BP's behavior can short-circuit the acting out.

Endorse a Paradoxical Position

The tendency for the BP to shift from one extreme position to another often makes decisions difficult. Dependency and needing to please, on the one hand, and angry oppositionality, on the other, may push the BP into commitments that she later retracts or is unable to maintain. She may declare one position on Monday, only to disavow it and grasp the opposite stance on Tuesday.

These back-and-forth decisions can be confusing for the partner who is uncertain how best to help. Sometimes, after several episodes of seesaw pledges and revocations, you can assume a contrary truth stance, in contrast to what may be expected. Endorsing an alternative, opposite to what the BP expects, may provoke a confounding reassessment of the situation. She may then undertake a more thoughtful, realistic evaluation.

> Norman, twenty-three years old, had enrolled in, then dropped out of, three colleges four times. Norman's pattern was to ambitiously take on a heavy load of credits, then get behind, and after a few weeks stop going to classes, isolating in his dorm room. His parents did not learn of this behavior until the end of the semester, when he confessed his grades were all "Incomplete."
>
> After initial anger, his parents would encourage him to return to school, recognizing his high intelligence and insisting he would be a failure without further education. Finally, they took a different tack. After several months living at home, where his parents avoided the subject, Norman suggested he wanted to apply to a new school and pursue a different major. His parents, instead of encouraging him, this time adopted a different posture. Although they felt that Norman ultimately would and should further his formal education, they now portrayed to Norman a contrary position. They suggested to him that perhaps he did not need a

degree. They avoided citing his previous attempts as failure, but they noted others who were successful without higher schooling. They asked him about interest in a job. They hoped that this line of dialogue would relieve Norman of feeling pressure for school and also cause him to more seriously question his motivation and consider alternatives.

It was a no-lose proposition: either Norman would become more independently motivated and more seriously return to college, defying his parents' paradoxical suggestions; or these considerations would resonate with his hesitations and he would avoid another failing attempt. Ultimately, Norman decided to stop school. He obtained menial work at a sandwich shop. After six months in the frustrating job he was determined to return to college. Norman went on to receive his master's degree in electrical engineering.

Set Limits

Setting limits with a loved one is difficult, and it should not be done without careful consideration. This truth-based technique is only helpful if it is realistic, consistent, appropriate, enforceable, and, indeed, *true*. Limit setting is not a code for threats or punishment. It is only a nonemotional statement of what you can and cannot do. It is better to avoid a truth proclamation altogether than to state one that will not be imposed. If your divorced spouse will not cooperate with your child's curfew, don't try to execute it outside the bounds you control. If you really don't think you can move out after the next altercation with your lover, don't threaten it. Instead, devise an action that you feel you can really act on.

Twenty-eight-year-old Jimmy moved back home with his parents after failed relationships and jobs in another state. He occasionally went out with friends, but at home he spent most of his time in his room, refusing to participate around the house or to make future plans. His parents pleaded with him to be more engaged, but he ignored their requests and threats. Finally, they agreed to approach him in a different way:

"Jimmy, since you have moved back home during this difficult time in your life, I want you to know that your parents will always support you and try to help (SUPPORT). We understand how hard this has been for you (EMPATHY). But we also do expect you to be responsible and pay the 'rent' we are requiring (TRUTH). We don't mean money. The rent we are charging you is the commitment to cut the grass each week, so we won't have to pay the gardener. We will also present you with a list of weekly chores. If, after one month, you have decided not to pay this rent and we can't negotiate a different relationship, you will leave our house and find another place to live, where you are willing to pay the rent."

Jimmy's parents expressed their support and empathy while simultaneously proposing limits. They must be prepared, however, to follow through and be willing to reinforce the truth demands. They must anticipate how they will enforce the limits and the potential consequences of their actions. These preparations include, if necessary, signifying a specific date for Jimmy to leave the house, obtaining assistance from the police, and consenting to the less pleasant alternatives for Jimmy.

Procrastinate Constructively

The BP can be very demanding and impatient. She lives in the *right now*. There may not be context for what is being experienced *right now*. What came before or may occur later does not influence what the BP feels at the moment. Current conceptions and feelings must be addressed *right now*. In turn, you may feel pressure to respond to these demands *right now*, even though any response may be countermanded, disavowed, or denigrated. Especially when the interaction is stressful, it is often better to postpone your response. Stalling may infuriate the BP, but it avoids your responding before fully considering the consequences.

These are some useful stalling phrases to avoid a commitment that later may lead to greater difficulty: "I know this is important to you, but let me look at my schedule first." "I'll get back to you." "I'll have to see if I can rearrange some things." "I hear your concerns, but I need to think if I can arrange it." "Hold on a minute. First let me return this call [or finish the laundry, or put away the dishes, or some such]." Preceding these truth statements with support and empathy acknowledgments can diminish the BP's frustration.

Barry insisted that his girlfriend, Shari, accompany him on his trip home to see his family for Christmas. She knew from past experience that these visits were fraught with conflicts. Usually, Barry would end up in a fight and leave early. She also knew that the family often blamed their relationship for the problems, and Shari became the scapegoat. This allowed Barry and his family to reestablish a temporary, fragile affiliation that excluded Shari.

If Shari rejected the invitation, Barry would be disappointed. If she agreed and backed out later, he would be even angrier. But if she went, she assured herself a terrible Christmas and again risked becoming cast in the role of the demon, whose exclusion unifies Barry's family. Her best response was to postpone her response.

Later, in a relaxed setting, Shari could reflect on her choices. She would first declare her wish to be with Barry and support him (SUPPORT). She would also acknowledge how important these family gatherings are for him (EMPATHY). Then Shari could decide to go with Barry, but with an opportunity to prepare herself on how to best avoid entanglement in the family dynamics. Or, after taking time to have produced a reasonable alternative, she could tell Barry that a family friend had asked her to spend Christmas with her this year, so she wouldn't be able to accompany him this time.

Defuse and De-escalate

The BP often interacts with others by denying his own feelings and projecting those disavowed emotions onto the partner. This is referred to as *projective identification*. He repudiates his experiences of anger, attraction, or confusion, attributing these sensations to the partner. If you absorb these projections, it reinforces the BP's denial of his responsibility in the interaction, since it is you, not he, who acts out the disavowed emotions. ("I'm not angry. You're the one who's angry!") This is an easy trap to fall into. It is important to recognize provocation and not get pulled into aggravating the cycle.

> Growing up, Krista always resented her big sister, Alicia. Alicia was a good student, an admired athlete, and popular in school. When Alicia would babysit for her, Krista would lie to their parents, asserting that Alicia was mean and irresponsible, talking on the phone and watching TV instead of supervising her. This caused Alicia to become angry, yell at her sister, and thus confirm she was "mean."
>
> As adults, contention continued. Krista insisted to their parents that Alicia was jealous and angry when Krista became engaged. When the women were together, Krista would raise her voice with accusations, provoking Alicia into louder refutations. "Well, I can see you're losing your temper again," Krista would declare and then withdraw.

When you perceive a pattern in which your "buttons are pushed," it is important to resist escalating the dynamic and acting out the projections. If the BP becomes louder, you should consciously focus on lowering your voice. If he becomes more animated, you should try to de-escalate by inhibiting your physical expressions. Support and empathy should be expressed using neutral phrasing. Exclaiming "Wow, you're really angry!" may only exacerbate the rage. However, less provocative empathy expressions can defuse the process: "I understand you're upset about this"; "This seems really distressing to you."

Don't Plow the Same Ground

If you find yourself continually repeating the same explanation, stop. Just as a child may continue to whine "But, why … ?" when a parent renders a decision, the BP may continue to argue the same point, which then arouses your frustrations. You might then feel pressure to either give in to the demands or pull away from the BP.

> After her painful divorce Krista asked to move in with Alicia. Alicia resisted the request, explaining that her apartment was too small, that she valued her privacy, that she feared it might strain their relationship. Still, periodically, Krista would ask again to move in. Finally, Alicia realized she was reiterating the same response to the same request over and over. She recognized her increasing anger at her sister, along with the temptation to either give in and allow the move or cut off contact. Instead, Alicia defused the interaction:
>
> "Krista, I know we've had this conversation several times (TRUTH). I love you and want to help (SUPPORT). And I know this has been a tough time for you (EMPATHY). But for all the reasons we've discussed, moving in with me is not an option. Let's get together and look at some other possibilities" (TRUTH).

By consciously focusing on supplying support and empathy, Alicia was able to control her anger at Krista. By offering truth options, she minimized guilt feelings and defensiveness, and she could stick to her limits.

Be Careful with Humor

The use of humor with the BP is dangerous and usually best avoided. The BP's exquisite sensitivity can interpret jocular light-heartedness as humiliating ridicule. Trying to inject laughter may appear to trivialize his feelings. It is best to avoid attempts to penetrate your loved one's serious concerns with humorous responses. Only in a long-standing relationship in which playful whimsy has been established can attempts at levity sometimes be helpful. In such cases employing a recognition of a kind of macabre, dark humor can help institute clearer perspective and can transform focused, frustrated anger into amusement that emerges from recognizing the larger context.

Bob and Carl's mother, Louise, was an emotionally fractured woman. Her husband died when the boys were young, and Louise was unprepared to be a single mother. She suffered bouts of depression and hypochondria that kept her in bed for days. These alternated with episodes of raging whippings. Live-in boyfriends came and left. The brothers learned they had to care for themselves.

Bob married and moved away. But Carl stayed behind and seemed to have inherited his mother's temperament. His two marriages failed. His hostile sarcasm pushed away friends. Intelligent and resourceful, he had no trouble finding work, but he became bored quickly and would move on to the next job. His temper, aggravated when he drank, engaged him in occasional fights. He maintained a hostile relationship with his mother, whose demands were frustrating. His brother was his only friend, the only person he could really talk to.

After another yelling match with his mother, Carl went to a bar. Following several drinks, he picked a fight with the bouncer there, resulting in a brief arrest. Carl called his brother to apprise him of this latest predicament.

"Carl," Bob started, "I know things haven't been going well for you lately, but—"

"Bob, you don't know the half of it," Carl interrupted, "and don't give me your condescending bullshit! You're a million miles away from Mom and all that I've had to deal with. My life sucks. Sometimes it just doesn't seem worth going on."

"I understand, Carl. You've been under a lot of pressure (EMPATHY). And this latest thing with Mom is classic. But, you know, if it weren't so upsetting, this whole episode, in a weird kind of way, almost sounds like a sort of situation comedy."

"It's not funny, Bob. I was in fucking jail!"

"Yeah, okay. And you know, Carl, how much I care about you and want to help (SUPPORT). But, come on. First, Mom calls you and for the umpteenth time says she has chest pain and is dying, and you need to come get her and rush her to the hospital. And then she says she can't go just yet, because she needs to put on her makeup and find those missing earrings. And, no, don't call an ambulance, because the siren gives her a headache and she doesn't want the neighbors to think she's sick. And so then you get pissed and go to the bar and pick a fight with a guy twice your size. And the police come with even bigger guys, and you smart off to them. And then...what'd you say to them?"

"Yeah, I said, 'I see the gun and the nightstick and the Taser, but only two cops? Where's the tank?'"

"Good one!"

"Oh yeah. I'm so tough. I put up my fists like we're going to spar. They just laughed."

"Sounds pretty funny, Carl."

"I guess it was pretty ridiculous. I think Mom's still looking for her earrings."

They both laugh.

"But seriously," Bob said. "Don't let Mom stir you up like this. It's a lot better for you to laugh with me when you get frustrated with Mom than for you to get plastered and in trouble, just because she thinks she's dying again!" (TRUTH).

In this instance Bob was able to use his long-term relationship with Carl to defuse his brother's desperation. He initially expressed his support and empathy, lightening Carl's mood before later leavening with truth.

What Not to Say

In BPD words can be important. So far in this chapter, the techniques presented to confront borderline challenges have focused on what to say. But it is also important to be aware of what not to say, what approaches may inflame the situation. The BP can be very sensitive and intuitive. It is important to be careful how you phrase your reactions.

- *Avoid a derogatory description.* Offhandedly responding to a dramatic exclamation with something like a casual "Oh, that's crazy" will precipitate a rejoinder like, "So now you think I'm crazy." From there, you are off to the races, decomposing your phraseology, distracted from dealing with the real issues. Use words carefully.

- *Avoid directly challenging the BP's stance.* Immediately contradicting the BP's perception often merely invites more conflict. Statements such as "That's not what happened" or "I didn't say it like that" may result in more frustration than enlightenment.

- *Don't demean the BP's reaction.* Disputing the intensity of the BP's reaction becomes a distraction. Saying "It's not that big a deal" or "You're overreacting" will only result in an empathy-lacking debate that ends in an accusation of "You just don't understand!"

- *Don't dodge your responsibility.* Attempts to dilute your frustration with the situation by saying "I was only kidding" or "I didn't mean it like that" will sound like you're shifting the blame on the BP and will only inflame the setting. When appropriate, it is better to just apologize for the remark or behavior that resulted in offense.

- *Don't lie.* Having a lie uncovered undermines all credibility and trust. Emphasize support and empathy when telling the truth as gently as possible.

- *Don't convey insincerity or pity.* "I feel so sorry for you," "You poor thing," "I know just how you feel" are phrases to avoid.

- *Don't compare your experiences.* Expressing empathy is acknowledging the BP's experience that is unique to her. It's not about you. Statements like "That happened to me, too" or "What I went through was just as bad" will feel dismissive.

- *Don't assume a know-it-all, fix-it stance.* Suggesting what to you seems an obvious solution that should fix everything will usually be rejected and may even provoke more frustration. Such a proposal—"Well, why don't you just call your girlfriend, say you're sorry, and bring her some flowers. That always works for me"—will seem haughty and oversimplified to the BP. Usually, he has already considered many of your suggestions, but, without more foundation and support, he may feel unable to carry them out.

Action Steps

Prepare/practice.

Preparing for a confrontation can be helpful. Rehearse what you might say and anticipate what the BP will say or do. Try to anticipate various scenarios.

> Frank knew that Alice would be angry. He had called 911 after she told him she had overdosed on her antidepressant. She had fought with the paramedics who took her to the hospital. When he visited her there, she was still angry at him for the call. After two days in the hospital, she was discharged, and he was about to pick her up. He knew she would minimize her overdose and accuse him of overreacting. On the way he rehearsed how he would approach her.
>
> He was prepared to avoid being pulled into an angry fight. When she yelled, he would keep his voice low. He would not interrupt but would let her ventilate. He would anticipate her defensiveness. He prepared SET responses: "I know you're upset with me, but I'm just glad you're feeling better" (SUPPORT). "You had to be pretty upset when you took the pills, and it sounds like you had a hard time in the hospital" (EMPATHY).
>
> Frank would save for later, when Alice was calmer, addressing the truth issues. He could then explain that her overdose had frightened him and that he would do whatever was necessary—even if it upset her—to ensure she was not in danger.

Be aware and accepting of your own feelings.

You are human. You will get frustrated. You will get angry. Count on it. Don't try to hide from these feelings when they emerge. Just be aware of them and do your best to compromise the impulses.

When you catch yourself raising your voice, try to slow down and talk softer.

Notice when your muscles get tighter when upset, and try to relax them.

Breathe. When feeling emotional, be aware of your breathing and slow it down.

When necessary, walk away.

Frank sometimes found it difficult to feel in control when Alice became angry or when she demanded he respond to her request. When he caught himself raising his voice and repeating himself, he knew he had to withdraw and to delay any decisions. He also could predict that Alice would accuse him of being a coward and running away from their problems. He would anticipate her response:

"I really need to step back for a bit. I know you're upset (EMPATHY), and I really want to work this out with you (SUPPORT). But right now I'm going to take a walk. Now, I know you're going to say that I'm running away, but if I stay, I'll get angry and defensive, and that will upset us both even more, and we'll get nowhere (TRUTH). Let's continue this when I can settle down."

Give a transitional representation of yourself during separation.

This can be a very simple but nevertheless effective way to ease the BP's anxiety and reinforce your bond.

After the divorce Martin missed the special times he valued with his teenage daughter. They both missed their frequent bedtime chats about school, girlfriends, and crushes. He suggested she keep a picture of him she liked by her nightstand. And he would do the same with her picture. They also picked out a particularly bright star to look at each night before bedtime to feel closer.

Recommend alternatives to destructive behaviors.

Writing in a diary may defuse frustration at others and avoid regrettable impulses.

Self-harming tendencies may be substituted with less hurtful activities. These alternatives replace damaging pain with less destructive discomfort, such as exhaustive exercising, beating on drums, holding ice cubes, and marking up skin with crayons or markers.

◗

Utilizing some of the strategies outlined in this chapter in conjunction with SET-UP should help you maintain a productive interaction and avoid or respond to the obstacles that interfere with open communication with your loved one. The following chapters in the next part of this book address common, familiar dilemmas in BPD. Employing the approaches described in the preceding chapters can help you effectively respond to these dilemmas.

PART
TWO

BORDERLINE
CHALLENGES

CHAPTER 4

The No-Win Dilemma

One of the most difficult communication obstacles in dealing with your loved one with BPD is confronting "no-win" dilemmas. How, for instance, should you answer the question: "Does this dress make me look thinner?" If you reply, "Yes, you look thinner in that dress," you'll likely be met with: "Oh, so, you *do* think I'm fat!" And if you say, "No, you look fine," the retort would be something like, "So, you really don't care what I look like!"

This chapter examines how to deal with what I'll call "damned-if-you-do, damned-if-you-don't" confrontations. The no-win situation is often your most frustrating challenge in addressing borderline paradoxes.

The Kobayashi No-Win

Surfacing from the BP's floundering sense of identity are perpetual contradictions. Confusion over what he needs is confounding, and although he may put the burden on you to meet that need, he may also resist or contradict the very intervention he requests. Such contradictions look like this:

- In a marital session Mary tearfully turned to her husband, Ray, and exclaimed, "You never show affection. I need a hug." When Ray stood up and embraced her, she recoiled, yelling, "Ouch! You hug too tight!"

- A few minutes into her phone call to him, Marcellus noticed that Angela's words were slurring. She responded to his concern by admitting that she had taken a few extra sleeping pills. Alarmed, Marcellus announced that he was calling 911 and coming over. Angela became furious and told him that she just wanted to go to bed and that if he came over or called for help, she would never talk to him again.

Dealing with your loved one's contradictory emotions can feel like a contest you cannot win. I have referred before to this damned-if-you-do, damned-if-you-don't process as the "Kobayashi Maru paradigm," a reference from the *Star Trek* television/movie series. In the show a computerized combat simulation to test recruits for promotion was rigged so that every action would fail, no matter what response was employed. (Captain Kirk became the first admiral to succeed by secretly rewiring the computer program before he was tested.)

The Black-and-White World of BPD

Helplessness, rage, and insecure fears of abandonment may all result in borderline behavior. The BP's black-and-white view of the world makes it difficult for her to commit to a consistent course of action. In a worldview of extremes it is hard for your loved one to pick a side, since every side has some contradictory elements. If the perception isn't perfect, it is terrible. Wonderful may mutate into horrible. Words contradict behaviors; behaviors contradict words; both contradict each other. She will reject all proposed solutions. Indeed, the BP may even "switch sides," adopting the opposite position to resist your intervention. She yearns for uncomplicated solutions. This can affect your relationship.

Because of the BP's anger and frustration, he often may paint a negative coating over what he considers your responsibility for the strained relationship. In such a way he perceives you, not himself, as the "bad guy." This often subconscious process is an example of projective identification. As described in the previous chapter, this defense mechanism emerges from the tendency for BPs to engage in splitting, in which people and situations are viewed in extremes of all-good or all-bad. In projective identification the BP denies his own dissatisfaction and projects it onto you, then manipulates your comments to reinforce the presumed hostile relationship. Then, as you become more frustrated and raise your voice, the BP, disavowing his own anger, can declare, "See! I knew you were mad at me!" Thus, the perception that you are the problem and he is blameless is preserved.

The complexities of a world filled with vague gray are frustrating for many of us. All-or-none extremes are generally more appealing. Children's stories avoid ambiguities. Good guys wear white. Bad guys wear black. We're drawn to the ideas of the TV counselor who solves the family's problems within the show's one-hour time frame and the dating show that pledges true love by season's end. With maturity, most of us can adapt to a world in which the color of the hat doesn't purely define the situation. For the BP, this advancement from childhood simplicity is harder to conceive.

Coping with the No-Win Challenge

A major part of coping with this dilemma is to first understand when you are entangled in it. The UP (understanding, perseverance) portion of SET-UP may help the interaction. Once you comprehend the situation, you can understand that no reaction is often the perfect one, as no response will be totally satisfying. Unlike Captain Kirk, who told Spock, "I don't believe in the no-win scenario!" and was able to manipulate the system, you may be less successful.

If obvious responses merely inflame the conversation, you need to back off. If you catch yourself more than twice repeating the same logical pleadings countered with the same resistance, you should abandon that tactic. When unfiltered truth statements result in no-win responses, you must consider a different approach.

- You can deflect the solicitation by evoking an opinion from the BP first. "I'm not sure how I feel about that. What do you think?"

- You can stall. "I'm so sorry. I'm very distracted [with work, with this project] right now. I'll have to get back to you."

- With a generous seasoning of support and empathy, you can expand the truth to acknowledge and explicate the damned-if-you-do, damned-if-you-don't dilemma, and propose a perhaps imperfect solution: "Honey, I understand how important family is to you and how hard you work on keeping family bonds (EMPATHY). And I want to support you in every way I can (SUPPORT). But almost every time your sister comes for a visit, she is very critical of you. And you've gotten mad at me for defending you; last time you were mad because I just sat there and didn't say anything. Since I'm afraid you'll be upset with the situation and with me no matter what, I think it best if I just excuse myself after a few welcoming pleasantries (TRUTH). Is that okay with you?"

- Finally, you must accept that sometimes the BP will need to be angry and hurt, and you may be the safest target for those projected feelings. In such a situation you must try to stay patient and sidestep the temptation to explain or deny accusations or exaggerations. You want to avoid, as much as you can, falling into the projection identification trap of reflecting her anger with yours. It may be best to absorb this upset without attempting to defend yourself.

A No-Win Partner Dilemma

This couple demonstrates the development of no-win communication:

> As Stella pulled into the driveway after law school classes, she was surprised to see that Owen's car was already in the carport. Walking into the house, she found Owen sitting in the dark, sobbing.
>
> "Owen! Are you okay? Are you sick?" She rushed to the table and sat down. "What's wrong?"
>
> "I couldn't take it anymore. Bill is such an asshole. I know it's his company and he can do what he wants, but he's ruining it. He won't listen to me. And I won't be a part of it."
>
> Stella had heard these complaints before. "Yeah, he's a jerk. But what the heck. Nothing you can really do about it," she said breezily.
>
> "I quit. That's what I did. I told him to fuck off and shove it." He cried harder. "I don't know. We've got our mortgage payment coming up, and your tuition, and...oh, hell, I don't know what we'll do."
>
> Stella was shocked. "Well, I'm sure you could call Bill back and explain—"

"No! You're not listening!" Owen spat out. "He's an ass. I'll never go back there. And I'm tired of this programming crap anyway."

"But, Owen, what are we going to do? You just said it. We bought this house. I have school…"

"Is that all you care about? The money? Your precious law school?" Owen's sad tears were mixing with fear and anger.

Stella felt her emotions bouncing along with Owen's contradictory attitudes. At first she felt surprise. Then compassion. Then fear. Now she was in anger mode.

"Owen," Stella implored, trying to stay calm, "we've got bills to pay. Maybe you could look for something else."

"Don't you get it? I'm not going back there. I'm not looking at computer screens anymore. I just don't care. And if all you care about is the fancy house you made us buy and your big-shot lawyer stuff, then you can just move on, because you don't give a damn about me."

"Look, I'm just trying to help," Stella retorted. She was yelling now. "I didn't get us into this. You wanted the house too. You used to like your job. You're blaming me for everything. If you want to quit, fine! I'll leave school and look for something."

"Oh, sure!" Owen replied. "You're just going to throw away law school after all this time and get a job. And then I can just sit at home and suck my thumb! How do you think that would make me feel? How would that look to everyone? 'Poor little Owen. Can't take care of his family!' You know, you would be a lot better off without me."

"Well, for God's sake, Owen, do *something*! Don't just get mad and feel sorry for yourself."

"I told you. I don't know what to do. Stop nagging me. Just leave me alone!"

A SET Approach to the No-Win Partner Dilemma

Navigating the damned-if-you-do, damned-if-you-don't voyage can be hazardous. The BP may threaten destructive behavior, yet demand to be left alone. In a crisis confrontation, part of a helpful response is to illuminate the contradictions in the BP's feelings and reassure him that you will respond in the most appropriate, most logical (Mr. Spock this time!) way. You can point out the opposite messages and explain that you will respond to the one that reflects true caring.

In the no-win operation Stella is locked into with Owen, he fights any attempt she makes to intercede. But if she can hold in mind the SET model, she may be able to confront this interaction more favorably. Here's a SET approach to how she can communicate with Owen once he's told her he quit his job.

Stella: "Oh my God, Owen! You must be feeling terrible" (EMPATHY).

Owen: "Well, of course I feel bad. That's a stupid thing to say. This puts us in a terrible bind. How are we going to pay our bills? I don't know what to do. I just know I'm not doing this anymore. Why don't you come up with something!"

Stella: [offended by his lashing out, but avoiding defending herself] "I'm worried about you and want to help (SUPPORT). We can figure this out."

Owen: "Oh, sure. What do want me to do? Call Bill back and beg for my job? No way. Maybe it's time for the princess here to wake up. Maybe you don't need to be in your fancy law school. Maybe we need to get rid of this stupid house you wanted."

Initially, Stella is tempted to defend herself again, but she quickly recognizes that this would be a diversion from the real issues and would distract them from approaching the crisis. It would also propel projective identification, eventually turning herself into the angry participant.

Stella: "Oh, so now all this is my fault... Owen, I love you. I just want to help" (SUPPORT).

Owen: [not absorbing the support message] "You have no idea what it's been like, working for that jerk. Day after day. Just for the cash. I'm the one who's had all the pressure to take care of us while you're in school. You'll never understand what it's been like."

Stella: [emphasizing empathy] "I can't imagine how bad it must have been. For you to finally cuss him out and walk off... Well, you had to be pretty upset today. I know it's been building for a long time."

Owen: [beginning to cry] "I just couldn't take it anymore."

Stella: "What do you think we should do?" (TRUTH).

Owen: "I don't know and I don't care. Get off my back. I've got enough to worry about now."

Stella: "I'm just trying to—"

Owen: [not receiving the empathy message] "Look! Your nagging isn't helping me. All you care about is school, and I'm just your tuition check."

Stella: [combining support and empathy] "Owen, I love you. I do know it's been a hard year for you. I feel you pushing me away, but we also know that this is something we need to face up to together. So let's talk."

Owen: "Talk? I don't know what to say. I don't know what to do. You can't help me. You should just walk away. You'd be better off. Just leave me alone!"

Stella: "I can see you're upset and angry at everything, including me (EMPATHY), but you and I have gotten through tough times before. We've conquered demons in the past, and we can adjust to this."

Owen: "I don't know what you want me to do."

Stella: "I want you to know that I love you and that I'm not going anywhere (SUPPORT). I will be with you, and together we'll figure out what to do next, just like we always do. Let's take a break and have some dinner. Then we can sit down and figure this out. There are some things I can do. I can look at tuition assistance, maybe a part-time job at the university, or even take a leave of absence. And there may be some things you can consider (TRUTH). For now, let's eat. I'm hungry."

Note that Stella realized early on that she couldn't confront Owen too bluntly with truth considerations during this crisis time. But she also didn't want to collude with his denial and anger. Her compromise was to emphasize her support and empathy for her husband, but also to insist that the truth of the situation must be addressed eventually, at a time when the acute upset over events has settled.

The No-Win Emergency

Violence toward others in BPD is relatively rare, but threats of self-harm and suicide are more common. In some situations you may confront a contradictory confrontation that is life-threatening.

Tom, twenty-eight, had been dating Harry, twenty-four, for over a year. Tom, an attorney in a prominent firm, had never formally "come out." Harry, who was completing his PhD dissertation, had proclaimed to his friends and family that he was gay at sixteen and felt accepted. Harry's varied talents, enthusiasm, and unique and adventurous style enchanted Tom. Harry was drawn to Tom's intelligence, independence, and self-discipline. But what Tom perceived as Harry's childish drama and what Harry perceived as Tom's stubborn conventionality sometimes threatened the relationship. They split up and then reconciled several times.

Their latest breakup seemed more severe. After several days Tom tried to contact Harry without success. Finally, five days later, Harry called. Through garbled speech, Harry told Tom that he had overdosed on sleeping pills and was calling to say good-bye. He told Tom he wanted the last words he heard to be Tom's.

Frightened, Tom said he was hanging up and calling 911. But Harry objected. He told Tom that if Tom didn't stay on the line with him, he would leave the house and let the pills do their work, away from any help.

"If you truly care for me, you will respect my wishes. Otherwise, it would only confirm that our relationship was a sham," Harry said. Tom knew from past discussions that arguments against suicide, reassurances, and other approaches would be fruitless, especially now in Harry's intoxicated state.

A SET Approach to the No-Win Emergency

In the above scenario Tom found himself in the most extreme type of emergency no-win situation. What could he do? What *should* he do? His first priority, of course, was attending to the emergency at hand as quickly as possible, so—while staying on the phone with Harry—he rushed to his neighbor's apartment, quickly jotted down on paper what was happening, and asked the neighbor to call 911 with Harry's address. Tom kept Harry engaged on the phone, encouraging him to talk and allowing time for the ambulance to arrive. When Harry realized the paramedics were at his door, he became angry. Once Tom knew that help had arrived, he took the opportunity to transition to SET mode.

> "Harry, you know how much I love you. I will do everything in my power to help you (SUPPORT). I understand that you have to be in terrible pain to go this far—to refuse to see a future and to feel that ending your life is the only answer (EMPATHY).
>
> "Harry, you must understand that something had to be done. You said that if I called for help, that meant I didn't care about you. But if I just stood by and let you die, surely that would show I really didn't care. Either way, I would be wrong and uncaring. So I responded in the only reasonable way I could and called for help. I understand that you are angry with me. But as long as you are alive, we'll be able to rationally decide what to do" (TRUTH).
>
> At that point the paramedics entered the room. Harry was taken to the hospital where he recovered. Later, Harry and Tom reconciled.

In this no-win crisis Tom did not have time to delay or postpone. He explained the truth to Harry—that either choice would be unacceptable and that saving Harry's life was paramount—to compassionately and reasonably justify his decision.

The damned-if-you-do, damned-if-you-don't scenario is frequently observed in interactions with the BP. When you balance support and empathy with practical truth observations, you can try to avoid your loved one's natural inclination to respond with anger and defensiveness.

Action Steps

Don't always try to fix the no-win.

Unlike Captain Kirk, you can't rewire the system, because the system is a person, not a program. And this person you care about will sometimes demand, but not be content with, any response. You may not be able to sidestep the BP's demands and may feel compelled to directly address her concerns. Accepting that there may not be a satisfying answer, you should embrace the most appropriate response, which prioritizes safety, practicality, and discretion.

> Every time Jeff left town on a business trip, Sheila cried and questioned why he had to go. Each time he dutifully explained the truth: Travel was part of his job. He liked his job. The job paid well. But none of these explanations settled Sheila's crying and clinging. When he proposed changing to a job with less travel, she became angry. She accused him of "guilting" her over work he loved and of being selfish in his willingness to sacrifice their current, enjoyable lifestyle.
>
> Jeff finally recognized that he could not calm her anxiety. At each departure he would abandon truth explanations and endorse mostly support and empathy statements:
>
> "I love you very much, and I hate to leave you this often (SUPPORT). You are very brave to endure everything that goes on at home while I'm away (EMPATHY). As always, I will call you every night and be home as soon as I can, so we can enjoy our special time together."

Jeff stopped trying to resolve Sheila's insecurities. He recognized that his explanations would not cause her to change her contradictory attitudes toward his work. Instead, he let her know he understood and accepted her insecurities and would do his best, through support and empathy, to ease her anxiety.

Here's another take on addressing the no-win challenge with a no-fix stance:

> Whenever twenty-six-year-old Lori had a fight with her boyfriend of three years, Chad, she called her mother, Maude, to complain. Lori would ask Maude what she should do about Chad, but no matter what Maude said, Lori would become upset. When Maude suggested the relationship may not be good for her, Lori would cry and pronounce her deep love for him. When Maude defended Chad and questioned Lori's role in the disagreement, Lori became angry and proclaimed, "You care more about him than you do about your own daughter!"
>
> Maude recognized she was in a no-win trap. She tried to respond by asking Lori what she thought or by changing the subject, but Lori insisted on a response. Maude took the approach of presenting her predicament and describing how she could best handle it:
>
> "Lori, I love you. You're my daughter and my highest priority (SUPPORT). You and Chad have had your problems, and obviously, that takes a toll on you. Sometimes you just don't know what to do (EMPATHY). I know you occasionally ask me for advice, but I've felt all I do is confuse you more. You've said that at times it seems like I'm pushing you to break it off, and at other times you feel I'm blaming you. I love you and have known Chad a long time. I can't really be objective in this. So I'm going to step away from trying to give advice. Maybe you both might consider seeing a therapist who could really be objective about your relationship" (TRUTH).

Maude described her position in this no-win paradigm and explained her response. In this case the option she chose was to withdraw from the conflict. Since you often can't satisfactorily resolve the no-win situation, you can try to evade or ignore it. Or, if you feel required to respond, you can describe the unsatisfying choices you see that are available to you, then announce how you feel you can best react. However, whenever you answer with truth, be sure to leaven it with support and empathy.

Know when to end the debate.

Don't overexplain. Don't keep repeating the same argument. You may challenge an unrealistic position. You may justify your action. But recognize when emotions overrule logic. If the BP escalates the confrontation, if you're having the same dialogue over and over, further discussion is fruitless. At such a time you should try to end the discussion, even though it allows unresolved issues to remain on the table. You must wait to deal with the problems when the situation is calmer or has resolved.

Sixteen-year-old Kelly had always been protective of her mother. Cora was a single mother working two or more jobs to support herself and Kelly. Cora came from an abusive home and had lived on her own since adolescence. As a teenager, Cora's only happiness came from playing the flute in the school orchestra. This ended when she dropped out of high school. Now Kelly was her main source of comfort.

Early on Kelly sensed that at times she needed to mother her mother, who had fits of anger and crying. Kelly worked hard to maintain good grades in school, to help around the house, and to hold on to a part-time job. When Cora came across her old flute, she gave it to Kelly and insisted she take lessons. Kelly complied, but she had little time to practice.

When Cora next insisted that Kelly audition for the school band, Kelly balked. She explained that, though she enjoyed playing music to relax in her spare time, she did not have time to join the band. Cora became angry. She yelled, then sulked. Kelly felt she was entangled in a no-win dilemma: If she refused her mother's demand, Cora would continue to alternate anger with withdrawal, and Kelly would feel guilty. If she agreed, there would be even less time for her to be with friends and to enjoy time for herself.

Both avoided further discussion for a few weeks. By that time tryouts had ended. Kelly continued to occasionally play the flute at home, especially when Cora was around. At Kelly's suggestion, both attended and enjoyed the school's seasonal concerts.

Kelly demonstrated support by agreeing to take lessons. She tried to acknowledge and exhibit empathy for Cora's connection with the flute. But logical presentations of truth ended in repeated arguments and stalemate. Continued discussions were futile. Kelly felt guilty over her mother's disappointment, but she accepted that she wouldn't be able to appease her without sacrificing her own needs. Kelly realized that by avoiding and stalling, the conflict would be resolved. She could comfort her mother by encouraging their engagement with the concerts.

Prepare your intervention.

Anticipate when interactions hit sensitive areas and prepare how you will deal with conflict. Anticipate your loved one's responses. Helpful steps include rehearsing SET principles in your mind, deep breathing, and adopting other ways to avoid losing control when your own buttons get pushed.

When Amy saw the suggestive texts to another woman on Matt's cell phone, she knew she had to confront him. First, she felt that she should just leave the marriage. Then she gave herself time to cool down and decide how to confront her husband. She figured Matt would be defensive at first, then angry at her "snooping" on his phone. She rehearsed her confrontation.

To soften Matt's expected initial response, Amy prepared support statements of her love for her husband and her certainty of his love for her. She then planned to inject empathy, stating her understanding that they both have been under a lot of pressure at work and lately have been frustrated at not having enough time for intimacy. She then rehearsed how she would approach her concerns.

Amy waited for a quiet time after dinner. She started by telling Matt that she saw he'd forgotten his phone this morning and had started to call him to let him know she had it. Then she saw the texts he and this woman were sending back and forth. She told Matt she loved him and wanted their marriage to continue. She said she needed to ask him how he felt about her and about this other woman. When he acknowledged his commitment to her, Amy insisted that he cease contact with the other woman and participate in marriage counseling. She acknowledged her hurt, but she wanted to work with him to heal this rift.

In an emotional confrontation it is easy to lose control. You may get angry. You may say things that only inflame the situation, rather than address it. You may get distracted by the BP's defensiveness or counterattacks. When you anticipate an emotional interaction with your loved one, it is helpful to prepare how you will approach it. Rehearse how you will address the situation. Anticipate how you feel he will respond to your statements and how you can reply. Having a script in mind will help you stay emotionally in control.

Use predicting to anticipate the reaction.

Based on past experience you may be able to predict how your loved one will react to a situation. This can help the BP understand her behaviors and demonstrate that what may seem to be unforeseeable impulses can actually be anticipated and understood: "You said it was okay with you if I went on another golf trip with the guys next Thursday. But remember how, last time, before I left, you started getting angrier and angrier? And finally, on the day I was supposed to leave, you got really mad and self-destructive. Let's talk it out now, so we won't go through that again."

Additionally, predicting the risk for dysfunctional behavior can stimulate an oppositional, but sometimes healthier response.

When Milton learned that his sister was in town and wanted to come by to drop off a birthday present for his son, he became alarmed. He knew that his wife, Bela, and his sister had always hated each other. Every time they were together, the mutual glares turned to nasty sniping and sometimes to loud arguing. Past entreaties to his wife to try not to get into a fight hadn't worked.

This time when he told Bela about the impending visit, he took a different tack. "I just hate to see how painful it is for you when you both get together," he told her. "I realize how horrible she's been to you. But I'm afraid you'll lose your cool again and blow up, and we'll have another scene in front of our son."

Bela turned some of the anger at her sister-in-law toward Milton. *How dare he tell me what I'm going to do,* she thought. *I'll be damned if I'm going to give him the satisfaction of doing what he thinks I'm going to do!* Bela responded to this challenge from her husband by being sickeningly sweet to their visitor, ignoring her sister-in-law's sarcastic insults. In order to counter Milton's offensive prediction, Bela resolved to act more responsibly.

Pointing out the patterns and the previous responses your loved one has exhibited can help her transcend *right now* reactions. Integrating past reactions and anticipating future attitudes can allow a broader perspective for the BP to understand how she designs a no-win dilemma for her partner. Truthful predicting should always be preceded by support and empathy statements. Detached pronouncements like "There you go again" and "You keep doing the same thing" will be resented.

Be consistent.

The BP's need to find black-or-white solutions to problems causes great frustration when contradictions emerge. Trust is difficult to establish. Limits may be constantly tested. It is imperative to give the BP what he is often lacking: boundaries that can be installed, maintained, and relied upon. However, don't establish a "red line" if you are not prepared to see it through.

> Paula and Mickey disagreed on what to do with their twenty-six-year-old son, Fred. After walking away from several jobs, Fred spent most of his time in his room in their home, where he had lived for the past five years after dropping out of college. Fred complained of depression and anxiety, but he refused to go for help. Mickey frequently would lose his temper and threaten to kick Fred out of the house. Paula would then tell Mickey to calm down. Everyone knew that Mickey's threats were empty.
>
> Finally, the parents agreed that something needed to be done. First, they needed to come up with a plan they could both support. They pledged their mutual resolve to see their proposal through. Together they sat down with Fred and told him that he had to get help. They would pay for treatment and, if he wished, would go with him to the doctor. If he refused to seek help, they would begin helping him choose an apartment and help him move out of the house. They would pay his rent for the first three months. They presented an exact date two months ahead, which would be his moving time if he refused their request. All of this was put on paper for Fred to see.

The most important part of providing consistency in this family dynamic is for the parents to agree on a plan. If one player subverts the stance of the other, the consistency necessary for truth to be absorbed and believed is lost. After agreeing to a proposal, Paula and Mickey needed to consider the contingencies and potential outcomes. They needed to anticipate and agree to a consistent plan they could follow that would encourage Fred, yet also accept the circumstances under which they would evict him from their home. To reinforce consistent limits, they needed to provide a time frame. They remained open to any amendments Fred might wish to offer. Paula and Mickey recognized that establishing a consistent structure with foreseeable outcomes was the best way to help their son.

Don't let projected feelings stain your own self-worth.

The BP may need to be angry, and you may be the safest target for that projected rage. The BP may constantly test your unconditional acceptance. But don't allow yourself to absorb all the vilification. Maintaining your own healthy self-esteem in the midst of condemnation is important not only for yourself, but also for the benefit of the relationship.

> After a long, contentious day at work, in which Larry and his boss had had a heated argument, Larry was furious that Howard hadn't yet started dinner. Howard tried to explain that he had been delayed and had just arrived home. Also, he hadn't heard from Larry, so he didn't know when he was expected home. But Larry would have none of that, remaining angry and complaining that Howard wasn't taking any responsibility in the relationship. Finally, Larry described the frustration of his day. It was then that Howard realized that his truth explanations wouldn't be helpful. So he turned to support and empathy.

Howard: "I'm sorry, Larry. I can tell that you had a terrible day at work" (EMPATHY).

Larry: "Damned right, Howard! And you're not helping any. I'm sick and tired of feeling like I have to do everything around here."

Howard: [avoiding retaliatory anger and recognizing the need for more support statements] "Let me help. Why don't you sit down and relax. I'll go ahead and whip us up something for dinner" (SUPPORT).

Larry: "No, damn it! I'm not hungry. I just want to be left alone."

After Larry stormed off into the other room, Howard reflected that in past situations, he'd continue talking to Larry at this point. But this time he understood that defending himself against Larry's unfair accusations would only aggravate Larry more. He needed to give Larry space rather than try to calm his anger. Howard needed some space, too. He was feeling battered. He had tried so hard to modify Larry's rage, and he felt beaten up for his efforts. He took time to think through the interaction and to recognize that Larry's angry accusations were a result of his upset, not an accurate representation of him.

Howard sat quietly, just breathing for a while. Then he prepared dinner for both of them and began eating. After a while Larry came back into the kitchen and grumpily ate. There was no further conversation until the next day, when Larry apologized.

Examine and respect your own needs and motivations.

It is okay to back away from the unwinnable. If discussion has stagnated, withdraw. Go to a different room, step out for a walk, take a drive.

It is okay to stall. Rather than succumb to pressure to say "yes" or "no," say "maybe" or "I'll think about it" or "I'll get back to you."

Examine your own need to rescue and be a hero. Sometimes, despite your best efforts, the relationship may not work. The BP may not molt and cast off the armor of illness that obscures the beauty inside. You may not be the one who can rescue the victim in distress.

The no-win dilemma permeates many of the other challenges that you face in your relationship with someone with BPD. Sometimes you will be knee-deep in the no-win before you recognize it. But once you do, using these strategies to disentangle from it will benefit both you and your loved one.

However, when the BP's frustration with the dilemma persists, erupting rage may be the most prominent feature to deal with. The next chapter explores considerations of borderline anger.

CHAPTER 5

Anger

This chapter examines ways to approach anger in BPD. Borderline temper presents differently than other angry behaviors. It is often sudden, unpredictable, and explosive. It may not be an observable, built-up progression of frustration. You don't see it coming down the tracks. The rails don't heat up, and there is no warning whistle. Suddenly, the train is in your face, loud and destructive. The BP can go from zero to one hundred, from ice to fire, in a flash, stimulated by what you may consider an innocuous remark or action. Shocking to the recipient, the sudden rage may be just as perplexing to the BP.

You may find yourself responding to the BP's volatile roller coaster of emotions—agitated rage to quiet isolation—with your own intense rebounds of emotions. Her fury may stimulate your defensive anger. And her withdrawal may cause you to recoil. Finding some middle ground between these extremes is best for both of you. When anger erupts in your loved one, and when you find yourself fuming in frustration, try to follow the advice of the twelfth-century philosopher and physician Maimonides, who authored *The Guide for the Perplexed*:

> With regard to all human traits, the middle of the road is the right path. For example: Do not be hot-tempered, easily angered. Nor on the other hand, should you be

unfeeling like a corpse. Rather, take the middle of the road: keep an even disposition, reserving your anger for occasions when it is truly warranted... This is the path followed by the wise.

Borderline Anger

Impulsive angry outbursts are observed in other illnesses, including bipolar disorder, substance abuse, and other personality disorders. But in BPD, anger emerges in a predictably unpredictable, consistently inconsistent pattern. When directed inward, self-harming rage may result in cutting, burning, substance misuse, dangerous promiscuity, or other self-destructive activity. This may be associated with depression. But when directed at another, it may be inversely related to depression; that is, projected rage often occurs with less feeling of sadness. If depression is sometimes anger turned inward, perhaps anger is depression externalized.

Anger may emanate from various sources. It is frequently a controlling mechanism, keeping the BP's partner always on guard. You may feel the need to pull back, convinced the relationship is ending. Alternatively, you may feel compelled to calm and reassure the BP. BPs with a history of mistreatment may employ anger as a defense against closeness, which has resulted previously in hurt. It may represent distrustful fears that you will inevitably bring harm to the BP. It may also guard against a fear of inevitable abandonment, pushing you away so as to "hurry up and get it over with." Expressions of anger may also serve as a kind of test of your commitment, to see if you can withstand the onslaught. Rage may convey a need to reenact severely contentious past relationships by stimulating more conflict, then turning it around: "I'm not upset. *You're* the one who's upset!"

The Explosion

Typically, you will experience the BP's anger as an outward eruption. You will be accused, convicted, and executed with cutting condemnation. Surviving the attack and maintaining the relationship can be a great challenge.

Stan, a busy attorney, was organized and meticulous. His wife, Marge, a teacher and mother of their infant daughter, prided herself on being more "spontaneous." She would sometimes playfully tease Stan's fussiness, but other times she'd become angry at his "obsessiveness." She alternated praising him for his promotions at the law firm with deriding him for putting work before family. Stan learned that Marge's reactions could change unpredictably at any time.

"Oh, good. You're home just in time for dinner," Marge said, smiling as Stan walked in the door.

"I'll be right there," he said as he followed her into the kitchen. "I have to make a quick call to this client."

Marge whirled around. "Damn it, I'm sick of this," she screamed, her eyes narrowed, her face flushed. "All you ever think about is your goddamned clients. Do you ever think about your family?" She began pacing in the kitchen.

"Okay, okay. I'll call him a little later. Settle down. Come on, let's have dinner."

"Forget it. I'm sick of this," Marge replied. "Work always has to come first. I don't want to eat with you. I don't even want to look at you."

"For God's sake, Marge. I said I'm sorry. But you know work is important. I work hard for this family. And, damn it, this job is what puts dinner on the table. So stop this crazy fighting and let's eat."

"So now you think I'm crazy."

"I didn't say that."

"Yes, you did. You said I'm crazy." She pulled the meatloaf off the stove and slammed it on the dinner table, breaking the dish. "Here's your fucking dinner that your job put on the table!" She stormed out of the room.

Stan followed after her. "Marge, I can't take any more of these tantrums," Stan, now frustrated and losing his temper, was yelling at a volume louder than hers. He trailed her to the bedroom, but she locked the door. Stan banged on the door. They continued hollering while their daughter, Allison, now awakened, screamed in the nursery.

It is a natural response to defend yourself against anger with explanatory truth statements. Stan's reaction to Marge's shocking outburst was to try to quickly resolve it with a quick apology and a truthful explanation. But in the heat of confrontation, explanatory or defensive truth will not be heard. Support and empathy expressions must come first. You must first accept and understand the sources of the anger, even if they are misguided, overemphasized, or even irrational. Marge's responses indicated her feeling that she was not being heard about the larger issue of Stan's commitment to the family. Her rage exploded. She needed to hear support and empathy messages. Stan lost control and tried to overwhelm Marge, with his own anger flaring.

Fire vs. Fire Creates More Fire

Fighting the fire of rage with more fire will usually not extinguish the blaze. As frequently happens, Stan lost control after he tried to cajole, explain, and argue, while Marge was in full-throttle rage mode. Keeping your cool is a monumental task, nearly impossible to accomplish all the time. But quickly recognizing when you are suddenly enveloped in the tornado can help sustain patience. Steering away from escalation and back to Maimonides's "middle of the road" is your goal. Speak softer when she yells louder. Talk slower. Inhibit your physical reactions. Avoid accusations. If possible, turn the attention away from the immediate dispute and refocus on an area less volatile.

Be prepared for further provocation, because your loved one may need to keep the fire burning and will be frustrated if you don't contribute more gasoline. Acknowledge her frustration, but delay meaningful responses until there is calm or exhaustion. This may develop through disengagement or emotional release through tears. Don't try to fix the crisis during the tirade, but acknowledge its relevance. Attempt to delay final resolution for a later, less stormy time.

Stan could more productively address Marge's rage. He should listen for indications that Marge requires from him more support or empathy statements when she is not feeling understood. Truth declarations will be heard only later, at a calmer time.

Stan: "You're right, Marge. The call can wait. I need to spend time with you at dinner and with Allison when she wakes up" (SUPPORT).

Marge: [screaming] "You always do this, Stan, and I'm sick of it. I have dinner all ready, but your mind is always on work, never on your home or on us. And then you say you're sorry like that makes it okay. I've had it with you, Stan."

Stan: [waiting to speak until an agitated Marge slows her angry pacing in the kitchen and glares at him] "I'm sorry, Marge. I've been so caught up with things at the firm that I haven't been sensitive to what you've been doing. It's got to be hard on you with work, taking Allison back and forth to the sitter, then coming home, making dinner and everything" (EMPATHY).

Marge: [beginning to tear up before her anger flares again] "Yes, Stan, it's been really hard. It's really hard. And you aren't helping one bit."

Stan: [not reacting to her recoiling from him when he tries to reach out to comfort her, but instead recognizing the need for more support] "I can do better. I will do better. But what's most important to both of us right now is asleep in the next room. We don't want to wake her up. And I know being a good mother is the job most precious to you (EMPATHY). After dinner let's talk about how I can help more and what we can do to make things better for Allison and for all of us."

Stan was able to stay patient and not retaliate. He delayed immediate responses, waiting for initial rage to dissipate. He used support and empathy to try to soften the interaction. He didn't try to defend or fix Marge's anger. He redirected attention to their sleeping baby, intending to tone down her yelling and to emphasize the importance Marge places on her self-image as a good mother.

Delicate Anger

Sometimes anger is not represented by explosive outbursts, but in more subtle ways. You may experience constant "constructive" criticism, sarcastic comments, belittling of ambitions and achievements. The BP may deny his anger in various ways: "I was just kidding." "You're too sensitive." "You're overreacting."

When his rage is out of control and way out of proportion, you can more easily rationalize it as his extreme behavior, less connected to you. But when he expresses anger more subtly, his declarations seem more justifiable. You may not recognize that his "trying to help" or "just being honest" remarks are really angry, resentful attacks. Instead, you may accept his self-representation as a concerned innocent who is only trying to help you atone for your missteps. "Constructive" assessments from the "wounded"

BP portray him as the victim, although they may serve to torment you. You may then find yourself embroiled in an elaborate sado-masochistic dance, in which who is punishing whom becomes blurred.

Nancy met Ryder at a USO mixer. Ryder was being discharged from the army and returning to his hometown, where Nancy worked at a day-care center. Ryder was shy but flattered by Nancy's attention, and they began dating. After his discharge Ryder found work as a carpenter. A skillful artisan, he began making chessboards, desks, and other fancy furniture, which he sold. After four months Nancy suggested they move in together, and six months later they eloped.

Within a few years Ryder's woodcrafting became locally recognized, and this side business flourished. Nancy was promoted to manager of the day-care center. She had several affairs, which Ryder suspected but were never talked about. In fact, over time, very little was talked about. They passed each other at home with the slightest of recognition.

Ryder first began drinking while in the army with buddies, but he stopped during the early years of his marriage. He used to like being drunk, but he feared it would upset Nancy. Now intoxication was becoming his main pleasure. After his second citation for driving under the influence, the court ordered him to rehab and then to attend Alcoholics Anonymous meetings. There he discovered a camaraderie that he had missed since his army discharge. He felt accepted and connected again.

Nancy's frustration with Ryder was expressed mostly in her withdrawal. When he showed her some of his wood creations, she would roll her eyes and offer "constructive" criticism or sarcastic endorsement. She would reject his sexual advances, then later question his manliness for not being more aggressive. But when Ryder began attending several AA meetings a week, she became more occupied with his activities.

Initially, she basically ignored his drinking, but now she was more critical. She called him a "weak pussy" because he needed alcohol to feel good. She especially criticized his dependency on his "feeble AA buddies." Why did he have to go out every night to a meeting? He should be enough of a man to stop drinking on his own and be home with his wife. Maybe, she insinuated, he preferred the guys because he was really gay and didn't know what to do with women.

Ryder's insecurities made him vulnerable to her increasing criticism. He felt beaten, but deserving of the beating. Pressured by her griping, he stopped going to meetings and ignored overtures from his AA sponsor. But now that he was home more, Nancy lost interest.

After a few months of sobriety Ryder began drinking again. At first he hid it from her, but later he knew she saw the liquor bottles in the trash. Like his vague awareness of her affairs, she knew, but she pretended she didn't. On some level she knew his failure at sobriety would be his punishment. But then it also became hers. One evening he appeared late and obviously drunk at an office party for her staff, thoroughly embarrassing her. This was the first time he had acted out his anger at her.

Ryder had absorbed Nancy's bitterness and affirmed her projections of worthlessness. He was unable to assert his feelings or contend with her provocations. Instead, he reflected her anger in his passively belligerent behavior at the party. In those moments their roles reversed: whereas before, Nancy was the sadistic punisher, battering the self-critical, passive Ryder, he now became the aggressor, humiliating Nancy. And their relationship then became more hostile.

Combating Subtle Anger

You may be susceptible to quiet anger, disguised at first as "helpful" suggestions that then subtly mutate into verbal thrashing. After a while the criticism may feel deserved, and your own self-esteem may be damaged.

Establishing firm personal boundaries will protect against too readily absorbing projected criticism. Let the BP know you have heard his criticism or accusation, but you need not endorse it, nor argue against it. Resist the BP's proposition that you are responsible for his contentment.

Ryder could have dealt with Nancy's anger in ways that would not have sacrificed his own needs. To do so, he would need to clearly demarcate his personal needs (speak the truth), while at the same time expressing empathy for how those needs might impact her, along with support and appreciation for her understanding of these requirements. He would also have to accept that he cannot be responsible for making her happy.

A more productive SET approach to their ongoing challenge might go like this:

Nancy: "Another meeting? This is the third this week. You're too dependent on your drunk buddies. They can't always be around and hold your hand and say, 'Don't drink.' Why do you think you need your little group all the time? Why can't you just stay home with your wife? You should be able to do this yourself. And a beer or two once in a while won't kill you. Don't be such a wimp. Be a man!"

Ryder: [resisting the urge to snap back] "Nancy, I understand you would rather I stay home. And I know you don't get why I think I need the program. But my sobriety is very important to me. And these meetings are really helping (TRUTH). I know it's hard on you when I'm gone (EMPATHY). And I do want to spend more fun time with you (SUPPORT). But for now this is what I need to do for me—and, really, for the both of us."

Passive Anger

Anger can also be communicated in quieter ways that punish you by inducing guilt or responsibility. Outward anger or frustration may not be signaled at all.

> Eloise was the youngest of three, with two older brothers. Her father was a large, intimidating man who ran a major manufacturing company. Her mother was a quiet woman who seemed to shrink in size when her husband raised his booming voice. Her older brothers worked with their father in the business. Eloise worked in the art museum gift shop, not far from the plaque citing her family's generous gift there. Before Eloise married Craig, she told him about her past history of depression and her temper, but Craig assured her their love would overcome all obstacles.
>
> Craig initially resisted his father-in-law's entreaties to work in his company and instead kept his job as regional sales manager for a chain of stores. But Eloise encouraged her husband to consider joining the family business. However, when he told her he had finally talked to her father and brothers and decided to join them, she became upset. She told Craig she was worried about his involvement with them. She told him how controlling her father was. She also shared that the reason she kept such a polite distance from her older brother was that he had sexually abused her when she was young.
>
> Craig was upset and uncertain what to do. He told Eloise he would withdraw his acceptance. But then Eloise changed her mind. She knew the salary would be much more, and

she told Craig he should take the job for the sake of his own career.

At first Craig enjoyed his work in the family business and felt rewarded for his good performance. But as time went on, the more he spoke about enjoying the job, the more resentful Eloise became. Now, after twenty years with the company, Craig felt trapped. He was financially secure, but he resented the limitations imposed by his father-in-law. Still, he felt it was too late to walk away. And as the years passed, Eloise became more embittered.

"Did you ever really love me?" she would question. "It's okay. You can be honest. Was it me or the money you wanted?" she would ask, crying. "I don't understand how you could work with those men every day, knowing how horrible they had been to me. All my life I've been hurt and abused, and I feel like it's still happening."

No matter how Craig tried to comfort her, Eloise shook and cried inconsolably. When he reminded her that, despite his reluctance, she had encouraged his entering the business, she responded that, yes, he was right. It was all her fault. When he insisted he would quit, she cried more. He started accompanying her to the therapist she had been seeing for many years. But Eloise spent the sessions attacking him. When her therapist challenged her accusations, she abruptly stopped seeing her.

"You're big buddies with my father and brothers," she complained. "You even ruined my therapy, so I had to quit. Instead of turning everyone against me, I wish you would help me. But I guess it's really not your fault. I have always been depressed. It will never change."

Craig felt more and more guilty and responsible for Eloise's unhappiness. He was constantly apologizing for every indictment. He granted her every request, hoping redecorating the den or getting a new car or moving to a bigger house would soothe the wife he loved. But Eloise continued to cry. New doctors and new therapists didn't help. Eloise would hint that Craig would be "better off" without her, which upset Craig more. He acknowledged his own depression and started to see a psychiatrist.

Craig loved his wife, but he was perplexed at how he could help her. First, he needed to accept that he couldn't easily fix Eloise. He also needed to recognize that she was oppositional to any attempts at soothing. She would either deny that his suggestions would help or she would halfheartedly attempt them, then tearfully declare them fruitless.

Eloise's passive anger was expressed by her demeanor of hopelessness. She punished Craig by frustrating his attempts to comfort her. To counter this, he started encouraging her devotion to their dog, Princess (a kind of transitional object, which she could love without fear of disappointment). Additionally, he learned to avoid making direct suggestions that she could easily reject and instead make more helpful support and empathy proclamations:

Eloise: "Craig, I know I'm just a burden sometimes. You'd be better off without me."

Craig: "No, Eloise. I'm your husband and I love you (SUPPORT). I would be lost without you. You have been going through this terrible depression. You surely feel hopeless sometimes (EMPATHY). But you're a strong woman, and I know you won't give up. We just need to keep working together and continue looking for help. I know how much you love playing with Princess. What are some other things we can enjoy?"

Anger, Outside In

Sometimes anger is turned completely against the self. This is a different dilemma for you. Instead of emphasizing shielding yourself, you may need to help protect the BP. Nevertheless, you are still challenged with confronting a fragile and often frightening emotion.

When Greg was growing up, rage was the aroma of his household. Everyone yelled at everyone. And Greg felt the discord was his fault. He was impatient and aggressive. He was just "bad."

In grade school Greg's impatience and fury was diagnosed as ADHD, and he was put on Ritalin. It didn't help. In high school he met Marilyn and fell in love.

Around her Greg reined in his anger, but Marilyn saw glimpses of it. She warned Greg that if they were to stay together, she would not tolerate his raging. But it was hard. One time after a disagreement he grabbed her arm and squeezed it until she cried in pain. She told him that if he ever did that again, she would leave him.

After three years of marriage, two young children, and demanding jobs, Greg struggled with the increasing frustrations of his life. Marilyn could tell when he was mad, but she didn't need to say anything because he would walk away and go in the garage. Usually, she would let him be alone there, but when she left the kids to check on him, she sometimes found him banging his head against the wall or stabbing his arm with scissors. When she tried to intervene, he would mumble, "I'm just a bad person" and resist her. It looked to her as if he were in a kind of trance. And, indeed, when he calmed down, he would sometimes remark that he didn't remember hurting himself. Only when he saw blood or began to feel pain did he "wake up."

Greg saw a psychiatrist alone first, then together with Marilyn. Stabilizing medicine helped modify his temper. They also devised a strategy to help when he felt angry. Marilyn would talk softly to him when she sensed growing frustration. They would sit in a quiet area away from the kids and dim the lights. Words of support and empathy were soothing. Marilyn kept a bowl of ice in the freezer. When Greg felt he needed painful stimulation, he would get the bowl and put his hands deep into the ice and feel the cold. Afterward he would write in his journal about what he was experiencing and what was making him angry.

Coping with the various manifestations of BPD anger is one of the greatest challenges to your relationship. Borderline rage can hurt you, cause you to doubt yourself, and batter your self-worth. It can make you feel guilty or responsible for the BP. The goal is to moderate the intensity of the conflict. Try to transport both of you to a calmer, less impassioned setting in which quieter consideration can be achieved.

Action Steps

Keep your cool.

Don't jump in with counterarguments. Wait for the BP to finish his tirade before you react. Avoid responding to his anger with a mirroring response of your own. Shouting louder than him just inflames the interaction. Countering his subtle criticism with passive-aggressive behavior prolongs the conflict.

Support, but don't collude. Be dependable, but not codependent.

You may understand the BP's position, but you don't have to consent to her portrayal or endorse her depiction of the situation.

Bianca was convinced that a neighborhood boy was bullying her five-year-old daughter and demanded that her husband confront the boy's parents as they walked down the street.

Bianca: "If you care about your daughter, you'll go up to them right now and demand that they punish their son for his behavior."

Umer: "Now, hold on, Bianca, I don't think—"

Bianca: "Umer, if you're too cowardly to stand up for your family, then I'll go out there and take care of it."

Umer: "Of course you're disturbed about this (EMPATHY). I agree that we both want to protect our daughter, and I am just as concerned as you (SUPPORT). But first we need to talk some more to Samantha. She just said the boy was 'mean.' We don't know quite what she meant. If he is causing a problem, I will call the parents and discuss it with them, but not in front of the children" (TRUTH).

Refocus the interaction toward a less charged area.

If angry passions cannot be eased, draw attention to a less intense subject or a subject about which you share mutual concerns. In a previous example Stan shifted Marge's attention to her devotion to their daughter. Another option is to target worry about how others may react to the conflict. ("I think our guests can hear us." "How do you think our family will react to this?") You can shift attention to a connected point; completely changing the subject will seem like ignoring the issue, but diverting to such related issues as the kids, the job, religious beliefs, problems with the house, or other shared obligations can lead away from dispute and toward cooperative considerations.

Emphasize support and empathy first.

An angry BP may not be able to hear truth until things calm down. First, show your loved one that you are both on the same page.

Hold on to your self-esteem.

Don't unquestionably absorb negative projections of who you are. When someone you care deeply for criticizes you, defames you, and questions your beliefs, it can be hard to maintain your self-worth. It is imperative that you have other positive influences in your life. You may need a trusted friend or counselor to talk to. It helps to say out loud to another person what stresses you are experiencing. Attending to hobbies, sports, or other satisfying interests can provide positive feedback. These other supportive individuals and interests can contribute a reassuring, uplifting balance to the sometimes exhausting strains in the relationship.

Fight fair.

Don't attribute anger to illness or medical condition. It will only inflame the situation without purpose to make statements such as, "It sounds like you didn't take your medicine today" or "You must be having your period."

Don't invoke confidential information in a disagreement: "You are just like your mother. You're probably going to get violent and abusive, just like you said she was." Such pronouncements can be seen as betrayal and can crush trust.

Fighting fair does permit you to identify how the BP's anger is hurtful, however: "Other than wanting to really hurt me, why else would you say such mean things?"

Keep clear the boundaries that define you and separate you from your loved one.

Be aware of the limits of what you can provide. You can offer only so much support and empathy. Truth, the reality of the situation, may dictate the outcome, which may be outside your control.

●

Enduring the "I hate you" part of BPD is perhaps the most formidable challenge to maintaining your relationship with your loved one. It is important to understand that the BP's behavior is a symptom of his illness, developed as a mechanism to shield him from hurt. It is not entirely a debasement of you. Persevering through the assaults and knowing that they're not all personal will help you through difficult times. Using the strategies exemplified here can help. And, finally, understanding that over time the anger will likely abate can grant you the patience you need to continue your loving relationship.

The next chapter addresses the inverse of repelling anger—dependent fears of abandonment—and how to cope with this facet of BPD.

CHAPTER 6

Abandonment

The other side of alienating borderline rage is the fear of isolated abandonment. In fact, these two emotional expressions so often appear together that they informed the title of my first coauthored book, *I Hate You—Don't Leave Me*. A Demi Lovato song uses the same title, describing a girl who wants to be held, but not touched, and whose confused relationships end badly: "When they love me, they leave me," the lyrics declare.

Just as borderline anger may push you away, the BP's fears of being left may pull you crushingly close. Panic over being alone results in claustrophobic clinging. Often, you may be confused by contradictory demands: episodes of rejecting furor alternate with pleading neediness for reassuring closeness. Abandonment fears frequently result from past disappointments and early deprivation. These fears derive not only from anxiety over physical distance. Emotional withdrawal may also stimulate abandonment distress.

It is imperative to understand that such anxiety may be impossible to fully relieve. You may be tempted to believe the entreaties that you, and only you, can relieve the constant fears. It is always tempting to play into the role of hero. But no matter how much reassurance you provide, it may never be enough to completely and permanently fill the hole. However, it is possible to calm panic using techniques described here. And, over time, the relationship can move in a healthier direction.

You may experience the BP's fear of abandonment in a variety of ways. It may be reflected in neediness, attention seeking, destructive behaviors, or angry frustration. To prepare yourself to deal with it, you need to be able to recognize borderline behavior while also accepting your own needs, vulnerabilities, and limitations.

Neediness

The BP often exhibits a need for instant intimacy. This emerges from a long-standing sense of emptiness that yearns to be filled. After a brief, casual introduction to someone new, the BP may initiate frequent contact, sharing personal details that seem inappropriately brazen given the newness of the relationship.

This may soon be followed by an assumption of intimacy that does not exist. Her Facebook page, for example, stocked with pictures, may declare your commitment at a time when you feel you're just beginning to get to know each other. It may shock you when the BP declares, "I'll kill myself if you ever leave me" shortly into her involvement with you. Even once a continuing, committed dynamic has been established, your loved one may plead for constant reassurance that you will not leave.

It is important to recognize this accelerating intimacy in both long-term and short-term connections as borderline behavior, and to recognize your own personal constraints. If you are sacrificing too many of your own needs for too long, you may need to modify or pull back somewhat from the relationship, in order to preserve it.

> Kim always looked up to her big brother, Eugene. Three years older, he was caring and protective. Eugene was handsome, a good student, and a superb athlete. Kim was

shy, chubby, and less attractive. When Eugene left for college, Kim was forlorn. With him away, she felt alone. Her parents, who had doted on Eugene's accomplishments, seemed to hardly notice Kim.

Early in Kim's junior year of high school her mother was diagnosed with breast cancer and died the next year. Her father coped by spending more time at his manufacturing business. Although Eugene called frequently, he was absorbed with college studies and activities. Kim felt alone and deprived of any family connection. After graduation she began working for her father in a low-demand administrative position in the front office.

By this time Eugene had graduated from college and returned home to work in their father's business. He also announced his engagement to Laine, his college sweetheart. Six months after they were married, their father died suddenly from a heart attack. The abrupt loss of her father was frightening to Kim, but she also feared the loss of her brother to his new wife and family, which would push her farther away from her anchors. Feeling more alone than ever, she turned more to Eugene. Several times a day at work Kim would leave her office and go to the warehouse with fabricated questions just to be with him. "I forget what you look like," she would declare.

Kim insisted on more time with Eugene and Laine. She called or came over almost every day. She installed a "Friday-night ritual"—a "custom" she devised that involved her accompanying them for dinner and a movie every week. Being close with them, Kim contended, was "what Mom and Dad always wanted." When Eugene asked about her social time with friends, Kim replied that she had Laine and him, who were more important than friends.

In the beginning Laine was friendly and tolerant of Kim's encroachment on their life, but after a while it became more burdensome, especially when Laine learned she was pregnant. Eugene's frustration was amplified by Laine's complaints. But the more he tried to accommodate Kim's needs, the more she demanded more time. With Laine's increasing insistence for more privacy and concerns about a new baby joining the family, Eugene recognized that he needed to confront Kim.

Approaching Abandonment

You may have found yourself in the same position as Eugene— loving someone and feeling an understandable sense of responsibility for this person, but also needing to set limits on the relationship in order to maintain it. Eugene's first attempt to address his sister's fear of abandonment didn't go as well as he'd hoped:

At the end of a workday at the office Eugene approached Kim and asked her to sit for a few minutes.

"What did I do? Are you mad at me?" she asked.

"No, of course not. It's just that you and I need a little more space. It seems you're always around, and Laine needs some more alone time during her pregnancy."

"I knew it! Laine has always hated me. I could tell she was manipulating you, wanting me out of your life."

"No, no, Kim. That's not true. But both of us are feeling smothered. You're always at our house. It's too much. You need to have other friends, other things to do in your life."

"Family *is* my life!" Kim screamed, crying. "That's all Mom and Dad ever wanted—for us to be a close family."

"Kim, we will always be a family, but we're having a baby and—"

"Yeah, your new family. That's where I get squeezed out. With Mom and Dad gone, I have no one, not even you. You and Laine would love it if I just faded away and died. Then you wouldn't have to worry about me."

Eugene felt guilty, exasperated, and angry. "Damn it, Kim! We're just saying we need a little more time for ourselves, to prepare the baby's room, to be with our friends, just to be by ourselves."

"Fine!" Kim shouted, getting up from her chair. "I won't bother you anymore." She walked out of the office crying while Eugene just sat there feeling guilty.

Confronting Neediness

Eugene can handle the conflict differently. He needs to keep the focus on just Kim and him. Invoking Laine's position dilutes the interaction and diverts attention to Laine, who then becomes a scapegoat. And it avoids Eugene accepting his responsibility for the confrontation.

He also needs to negotiate specific, consistent boundaries. These might include establishing regular "private time" slots for Eugene to be alone with his family and informing Kim that there will be no more "surprise" visits. These clear limitations should be balanced by equally concrete solutions, such as scheduling a set "visiting hour" each week and arranging activities that everyone can participate in together.

Finally, Eugene should use more support and empathy statements to introduce the truth with which he is challenging Kim.

The same scenario as above might have gone far differently if Eugene had employed these techniques.

Eugene: [starting with support statements] "No, Kim, nothing's wrong. I want to show you something. Remember over Thanksgiving, when I was taking portraits of the three of us with the tripod? Well, I want to give you one. I think it turned out well. I love this picture. Everyone looks healthy and happy, and Laine is showing off her baby bump."

Kim: [excited] "Thank you, Gene! I know just where I'm going to put this—on the dresser in my bedroom, so I can look at you guys when I wake up and when I go to sleep."

Eugene: [drawing Kim into feeling like part of the family unit] "Well, we're really excited about the baby coming, and I think I know a good babysitter who just might want to help out."

Kim: "Oh, you know it. Aunt Kimmie's ready to go. I can't wait."

Eugene: "Neither can Laine and I. We're starting to make some plans. We're setting up the baby's room, painting and arranging furniture. So we're getting really busy."

Kim: "Well, you know I want to be involved. Let me help."

Eugene: "Kim, we need some nesting time. Just the two of us, to get used to feeling like parents. And with the baby coming, we're thinking about how we want to raise him. I know our family has never been particularly religious, but we decided we want to provide a Jewish home for the baby. So Laine and I are going to start going to Shabbat services at the temple on Friday nights again."

Kim: "But that's *our* Friday-night time."

Eugene: [expressing empathy and offering specific alternatives] "I know, Kim. We're trading that ritual for a ritual with God. And I know you're disappointed, but I thought we'd do something else instead. I figure we need a break from work in the middle of the week, so I'll take you to lunch on

Wednesdays. Maybe Laine and the baby can join us sometimes."

Kim: "That's not the same. I need that time with you."

Eugene: "I understand, Kim. This is different and change is hard (EMPATHY). But our life is changing with the baby coming, and I think that will mean changes for you, too—your role in the family (TRUTH). You won't just be a little sister anymore. You're going to be an aunt. The three of us are going to count on you to be strong and responsible. I need for you to have a life outside of just our little group. I want you to bring to us and our child your outside life, your different experiences, your world outside ours."

Kim: "Well, sure. I'll do that. But that doesn't mean things have to change so much."

Eugene: "I don't want you to get most of your strength through us. I need for you to develop new interests and activities. When you were growing up, you were a real good athlete. You were the best spiker in volleyball. The community center has a league I wish you would think about joining. And also getting back to the gym. Your nephew is going to need a good and healthy role model."

Kim: [missing the support messages] "But I still need time with you. You're just throwing me away."

Eugene: [reaffirming support, then pointing out that giving in to her dependency can stunt her growth] "Kim, I'm your big brother. I've always taken care of you and protected you (SUPPORT). I worry that maybe at times I've been too protective. You would come to me with a problem, and

I'd always try to fix it. And maybe I've kind of interfered with your need to learn to fix things yourself. You can't have a life that revolves solely around me and Laine and the baby. A circle that tight isn't healthy. You need to have your own life. And I'm stepping back. You need other friends, other supports, other interests. And so do we. We need to meet other young couples and families with young kids.

"You know you are always welcome as part of the family, but we need our own family time now too. I don't want you just popping over, whenever. Laine could be nursing, or I could need some quiet time. You need to call first. We may not always be able to set up regular times every week while we adjust to having an infant, but we'll always be a family and be together" (TRUTH).

Kim: [not absorbing the empathy, crying] "You're leaving me, just like Mom did, just like Dad did. You don't understand. I'll be all alone."

Eugene: "No, Kim. I will always love you (SUPPORT). I understand you are feeling bad and worrying about being left behind (EMPATHY). But that's not happening. We're just developing a new understanding of how we can continue to be a growing family with new roles for all of us—Daddy, Mommy, and Aunt Kimmie" (TRUTH).

For several months Kim had difficulty adjusting to the new limitations, but Eugene and Laine maintained the boundaries consistently. When Kim came to the house unannounced, they told her it was a bad time and asked her to return at a specific time later. One of them called Kim a few times a week for extended chats, but when she called them, they kept the conversation short. They continued to encourage Kim to widen her social circle, pointing out activities that might interest her. They invited her to functions where they could introduce her to others. For a while Kim slept with the framed picture Eugene had given her, but she later returned it to her dresser along with a more recent picture of her, Eugene, Laine, and the new baby.

This intervention succeeded because Eugene and Laine had planned it out ahead of time with knowledge of abandonment issues in BPD. Eugene first presented Kim with a transitional object (the framed photo). He emphasized support and empathy. He listened carefully to her responses to assess if she was truly hearing him and reemphasized support and empathy messages when they weren't getting through. He also understood that he and his wife would have to consistently enforce the new truth limitations they set on the relationship. They prepared how to respond when Kim tested those limits. Lastly, they instituted a new family structure that included Kim and that she could accept.

Close, But Not Too Close

Typically, you will experience the BP's abandonment anxiety as demands for closeness and reassurance. He may express a need for what feels to you like excessive snuggling and hugging. Sex may begin to feel like a compulsive ritual, rather than a spontaneous expression of love or lust.

But sometimes his fear of ultimate abandonment or engulfment may construct contradictory mandates. He may be jealous of your other relationships and demand an exclusive one with you, yet engage in flirtations or brief physical liaisons with others himself. This need to feel attractive to you but also to others represents a guard against desertion. The BP who struggles with abandonment concerns may feel the need to reassure himself that there is always another potential relationship "in reserve."

Such mixed emotions present significant barriers to establishing an exclusive commitment. In order to retain the relationship, you may have to accept borderline behaviors that orbit in and out of intimacy.

Charlene and Tanya met at a bar and were immediately attracted to each other. They were also surprised at how alike they were. Both emerged from troubled families. Both endured a string of unsatisfying affairs. They experienced frequent mood swings. Both had even seen the same therapist at different times in the past, laughingly acknowledging that he had been no help.

After spending most of their time together for several months, Charlene suggested they consider moving in together. But Tanya balked. She feared that cohabitation would become too claustrophobic, too confining. She was also afraid that if she became too familiar to Charlene, she would lose her appeal. Tanya wanted to be with Charlene, but not with her too much. If they got too close, she was afraid she would sacrifice her independence.

Despite Charlene's reassurances, Tanya was insecure about her attractiveness and sexual performance. After a while Charlene expressed her frustration with Tanya's constant need for consoling, which only increased Tanya's insecurities. Tanya was furious that Charlene remained friendly with other women, although Tanya maintained online sexual dalliances and continued an intermittent romance with a woman out of town. Tanya and Charlene would argue, break up, sometimes for months at a time, then reconcile.

Charlene finally understood that she and Tanya wanted different things from the relationship. They loved each other, but Charlene was ready to commit and Tanya wasn't.

She felt responsible for Tanya, but she saw that Tanya could not return the same devotion. Charlene recognized Tanya's need for constant reassurance from multiple people, but she tired of Tanya scurrying back to the comfortable safety of their on-again, off-again relationship after one of her excitement-seeking trysts. Following a serious fight, Charlene finally addressed the relationship directly.

Tanya: "I know you're mad at me. Please, Charlene, don't leave me. I couldn't go on without you in my life."

Charlene: "Tanya, I will never stop loving you. And I know you love me too. I want you always in my life (SUPPORT). But it's clear we want different things from each other now. I'm ready to settle down. But you aren't ready for that commitment. I understand how important it is for you to feel in control of your life. I think sometimes you feel claustrophobic in our relationship (EMPATHY). I need to let you be you, and we both need to accept that we're at different stages in our lives (TRUTH). And that's okay. I am not willing to give up our relationship. I accept what we have now. Someday I hope there will be a more complete commitment. But for now we don't have to fight so much if we just accept who we are together."

Like Charlene, you may be unable to fully assuage the BP's insecurities. In order to maintain the attachment, you may need to accept that full commitment may not be possible at this time. Like the gravitational forces between orbiting stars, you may feel a constant push-pull that keeps you connected, but not colliding; close, but not too close; committed, but not too committed. Such a relationship doesn't cure your loved one's abandonment fears, but it does allow you to remain in each other's lives at a level of intimacy that is viable for both of you.

"I Know You'll Leave Me"

The BP is on guard because of his fear that you will abandon him. He may be convinced that you will eventually uncover the real, unlovable him, then end the relationship. He may require constant reassurance that you love him and won't leave. Alternatively, he may continuously provoke you, testing you to see if you will pull away. This behavior can reach outrageously excessive proportions if he has already conceded a kind of "hurry up and get it over with already" posture.

In the beginning Lisa's comments to Max were said teasingly. When he presented her with earrings for her birthday, she said, "Are these like the ones you bought your mistress?" Following intimacy, she remarked, "Just hanging around so you can get lucky, huh?" After a while her statements became more bitter. During a minor fight, she said to Max, "If you're not happy, just say so. I know you're going to leave me. Why don't you just leave!" These comments would be intermingled with pleadings like, "You still love me, don't you? Please be patient with me. I don't want to lose you."

Max eventually realized that continual reassurances would never be enough to totally satisfy Lisa. So he confronted her distancing behavior in an understanding way that lessened the tension:

"I love you very much and treasure our commitment (SUPPORT). You've told me about the hurt you experienced from past relationships, and maybe you're feeling insecure about ours (EMPATHY). Sometimes I think you try too hard to please me, when you really don't have to. But lately, it seems like the opposite—like you're testing me, pushing me away, to see if I'll leave (TRUTH). You don't need to do that, either. I love you for you, and I'm not going anywhere" (SUPPORT).

In this instance Max understood that he is being tested to determine his commitment. He confronted the truth behind

Lisa's behavior while at the same time emphasizing his support for the relationship.

"Hold Me...Don't Smother Me"

The BP wrestles with feelings of emptiness and lack of a consolidated sense of identity, which is exacerbated by abandonment. But as much as the BP craves closeness, he also fears engulfment, being taken over and controlled. He can build a semblance of who he is based on a clinging relationship. If he loses the connection, he loses that facade. But, paradoxically, he can also lose that sense of selfhood if he abandons his own personality and is totally overwhelmed by his partner.

As the partner, you may become the target for this conflict. The BP's craving for merging with you conflicts with his fear of being controlled. He may alternate complaints that you are not paying enough attention to him with demands that you stop telling him what to do. BPD anger may emerge from this fear of being overwhelmed or consumed.

Since she was fourteen, Judy had been in charge of her family. Her mother was morbidly obese, her father, deeply depressed, and her sister, mentally disabled. Judy cooked, cleaned, and ran errands. She couldn't wait to get away to college. At home she felt used, yet invisible, as if she were a floating hologram with no flesh, no personality, no self. At college she felt she could develop her own, separate identity. She could learn who she wanted to be.

Judy became involved with the theater group on campus and discovered she loved acting. She could easily assume the persona of another. She could understand and identify with the characters she portrayed on stage. For the first time in her life Judy felt she fit in.

In her junior year she began dating Hal. When he proposed the next year, Judy was determined to be the perfect wife. This would be her best role. She decided to drop out of college, even though she had less than a semester to go to graduate. All of Judy's energy went into planning the wedding and fixing up the home they selected, near Hal's new job. They agreed that Judy wouldn't need to work. She would stay home modeling the perfect couple in the perfect house. Judy yearned to be the adoring and adored suburban housewife from the old black-and-white comedies—like Harriet Nelson from *Ozzie & Harriet* and Laura Petrie from *The Dick Van Dyke Show*. She would be whatever Hal wanted her to be, and he would be with her forever, just as it was on TV.

Judy gloried in her role. She made lunch for Hal every morning. She brought cookies to his office in the afternoon. She called him in the morning to ask what he wanted for dinner. He called her in the afternoon to thank her for the cookies and to say he loved her.

But Hal got busier after a recent promotion. He stopped calling in the afternoons. He was assigned work out of town. She called Hal's office several times a day, despite his requests to stop. When he was traveling, she demanded he call her during the day. When he explained he hadn't the time, she accused him of having affairs. Judy was being what she thought Hal wanted, but he wasn't playing his part. He was trying to change her and to control how she was supposed to feel. Judy sulked. She cried. She got angry. She got depressed. At Hal's insistence she agreed to see a psychiatrist.

Dr. White seemed kind and accepting. The antidepressant helped her mood, but she continued to feel lonely and frustrated at home. After a while she became frustrated with the doctor, too. He limited her calls in between their weekly therapy sessions. He resisted her "just one more thing" attempts to forestall the end of each session.

Judy feared her doctor was pulling away, just like her husband. It seemed *he* wanted to change her too. Judy kept his business card with her at all times. She would fondle the card's embossment when she felt abandoned, which soothed her. She presented him with a small figurine at Christmas, which he placed on his bookshelf. Seeing it there each week reassured her he cared about her, even as he tried to modify her dependency.

But the relationship with Hal continued to be strained. The more Judy cried and clung and raged, the more Hal withdrew. Then his anger emerged in ways she had never seen before.

"I can't take this anymore!" Hal bellowed. He had just returned from a trip out of town. Just as he had come in the door and put down his suitcase, Judy was crying that he hadn't called her since the previous evening. "I can't hold your hand every minute. Don't you understand? I'm busy. I have work to do."

"Why can't you call? You have time."

"No, I don't," Hal replied. "I have clients. I have meetings. I have a job. What is wrong with you? You need to get a life."

"Oh, so I should get a life!" Judy said sarcastically. "This *is* my life, living under your thumb, taking care of your house, and waiting for you to decide to come home. You just pull my strings and I dance for you, but if I ask for a little something, well..."

"This is nuts, Judy." Hal was exasperated. "Have you been seeing the doctor? Are you taking your medicine?"

"This has nothing to do with the doctor or the medicine. Stop trying to push all this on me. And I'm not 'nuts.' I'm your perfect little wife, who makes your meals and goes to her shrink and keeps her mouth shut. I do everything you want me to do. Everything is on your schedule, and I'm just supposed to fit in somewhere. Maybe if you paid more attention to me, we—"

"It's never enough for you, Judy. No matter what I do, it's never enough attention. I've had it!" Hal barked as he grabbed his suitcase and stormed toward the door. "I am not putting up with this anymore," he yelled, slamming the door behind him.

Judy rushed to the door crying. As she sunk to the floor, she yelled through the door, "I'm so sorry." Then she thought, *Where do I go? What will I do?* She wasn't Harriet Nelson anymore. She was Scarlett O'Hara, and Hal didn't give a damn.

Reassurance with Boundaries

There are steps you can take to constructively deal with the BP's expression of contradictory impulses, to allay the anxiety of abandonment while also encouraging independence. In Hal's case he is frustrated by his wife's alternating excessive clinging and resentment. Judy wants to grab on to a role she can play, which she hopes will grant her a sense of security. But she is angry when others don't fulfill their complementary roles. And then, after a while, she feels manipulated and resents the constraints imposed on her by assuming this identity.

Hal must accept that he may never fully satisfy Judy's demands. He needs to respond in ways analogous to how Judy's psychiatrist responded to her: He must reinforce his caring and dedication to the marriage, and acknowledge her needs. He can accept and help her with her abandonment fears. He can encourage increased independent activities to help Judy expand her sense of self. But he must also negotiate clear, consistent, workable boundaries within the relationship. He must temper the truth with much support and empathy.

Hal: "I understand you are feeling alone and upset. And I know how hard this has been for you these last months with my work demands (EMPATHY).

Believe me, I get how you feel, because I miss you too when I'm this busy. I love you very much and hate being away so often (SUPPORT). I appreciate how hard you work to make our home as warm as it is" (EMPATHY).

Judy: [not hearing the empathy] "Do you, Hal? Do you really appreciate what I'm doing to please you? I've given up everything for you. And you're just too damned busy to even call your wife!"

Hal: "I know it's frustrating for you (EMPATHY), but it's impossible to steal away when I'm going from one meeting to the next (TRUTH). But I'll tell you what I do that helps me when I'm missing you. See this picture of you in my wallet? In between clients I take it out and look at you. That makes me feel close. I can even smell your perfume when I touch it. Maybe something like that would help you."

Judy: "I smell you when I take your undershirts to the laundry room."

Hal: "It's very frustrating for you when you're waiting around hoping I'll find a second to call. You must feel lonely a lot (EMPATHY). Maybe you can find some more things to do in town. I think you'd love to get involved in that new community theater group or volunteer at the museum.

"But for now let's set up a system. There's usually no time for me to call during the day. And in the evenings I'm expected to take clients to dinner. Afterward I'm dead tired, but I'm normally back at my hotel by nine. So you can expect a quick call or text from me around then. Until I have a better feel for my job, that's the best I can do (TRUTH). And on weekends and time off, let's spend our time together and explore some new things you'd enjoy doing" (SUPPORT).

When you recognize that you are dealing with abandonment issues, you must understand from the start that you may not be able to assuage all of these insecurities. You can, however, encourage, reassure, and accept. In the process, balance the needs of your loved one with your own.

Action Steps

Summarize what is being said.

It is important for the BP to know that you comprehend the severity of his anxieties and the needs he is communicating. Restating his concerns in your own words demonstrates that you grasp what frightens him.

Use transitional objects.

Just like a child's doll instills comfort and companionship, a picture, a sample of clothing, a piece of furniture, or a small memento can symbolize your presence when you are absent (see chapter 3). You can also form a soothing connection by picking out a common star in the sky or agreeing to watch a particular TV show at the same time when you are apart.

Prepare for separations.

In BPD, experiences from the past may merge with emotions from the present, but anticipation and preparation for the future may be impaired. When tomorrow's plan becomes today's activity, the BP's response may be shock and upset, as if she were only now learning about it. You can counteract this shock by expecting it.

When Melanie was preparing for an out-of-town business trip, she would remind Mike every few days about her impending departure. For example, she'd ask him to help her pick which suitcase to take or to help her rehearse her presentation. A few days out she'd talk to him about what plans he could make for himself or with friends for when she was gone.

In the hopes of avoiding an angry outburst, she reminded Mike how mad he was last year when she went on a similar trip. By anticipating Mike's emotional response to her absence, she faced it head-on in advance, openly talked things out with him, and successfully deflected a conflict as she was leaving.

Encourage outside connections.

Helping your loved one engage in connections outside of your relationship lessens the conflicted dependency on you. Attending a class, joining a sports team, volunteering for a charitable cause—there are countless activities apart from your time together that can involve her with others. Outside interests become supportive anchors she can hold on to when feeling insecure. They also help protect her from feeling overwhelmed by you.

Accept your limitations: don't try to play doctor or be a savior.

Just as you must accept that your loved one may be incapable of completely filling his emptiness, you must also accept that you may be incapable of providing all the help you wish you could. It is easy to feel guilty that you are not doing enough, that if you just provided more support, you could ease his pain.

You must take stock of the capacity you have to give—how much time, money, devotion can you provide without draining your own resources? Recognize that any lingering guilt must be overcome by recognizing your own limits. There may come a time when you must inform the BP, as precisely as you can, what more you can provide and exactly what the limit is.

Phil and his girlfriend of five years were always fighting, breaking up, then getting back together. After every separation Phil, lonely and depressed, would call his best friend, Bruce, who would drop everything and immediately come over and try to cheer him up. Bruce was flattered that his friend turned to him for help, but Bruce's ministrations never seemed to help much, which left both of them feeling disappointed. Logical discussion of the relationship and how Phil might adjust his behavior seemed repetitive and fruitless. Bruce found himself repeating the same advice over and over. And Phil continued to insist that he couldn't make suggested changes.

Bruce finally accepted that his guidance was limited. Bruce adjusted his attitude. He would be supportive and sympathetic, but he gave up trying to "fix" Phil's insecurities. He told Phil, "I'm your best friend, and you know I love you. But that means I can't be very objective in trying to help. I know of some therapists who would certainly be less emotionally involved than I am. Let's look into getting you some real help."

Balance the boundaries.

Recognizing your own limitations will require an understanding with the BP of the expectations you have of her and of yourself. Don't make demands that will not be enforced. Frame boundaries as precisely as possible. Make sure expectations are understood.

Setting boundaries in the relationship is frustrating to the BP. Explain how your collaborating with the neediness interferes with her growth. In this way you share responsibility for the situation and lessen the need for her to blame herself.

Evan and his wife, Ava, couldn't refuse his brother Gary's request to move in with them. After Gary's job was eliminated the previous year, he began drinking. His wife had an affair with a neighbor and kicked him out of the house. Gary moved into their guest room and began looking for another job. But as the weeks went by, Gary became more discouraged. He stopped going out for interviews. He spent more time in his room and increased his drinking.

Ava felt sorry for Gary. Evan was getting angry and wanted him out of the house. Ava defended her brother-in-law, insisting he was ill and needed their help. When they approached Gary, he agreed he needed to stop drinking and look for work, but that pledge lasted only a few days. When Evan yelled at him over his lack of progress, Ava scolded Evan for threatening Gary. Now the problem wasn't Gary. The problem was that Evan and Ava needed to agree on how to deal with him.

With the help of a couples' counselor, Evan and Ava were able to concur on a strategy to deal with Gary. Together they sat down with him and confronted his alcoholism. They told Gary that they wanted to be supportive, but not so protective that he would abdicate taking responsibility for his behavior. They insisted that he enter a rehab program they had researched. Following discharge he could remain in their home for the next six months, as long as he remained sober. He also was required to be out of his room for their meals together. After six months (on a specific date they formalized) they would discuss future plans. Evan and Ava wrote out a specific contract detailing the agreement. If Gary violated the arrangement, he would leave the house for a homeless shelter that was available. Gary signed the contract and entered rehab the next day.

Your wish to stay close to the one you care about is hampered by conflicted insecurities of abandonment. The BP's wish for commitment is contradicted by his fears of being overwhelmed. Understanding and persevering with this paradox can help maintain the loving feelings you both have.

Abandonment fears are related to feelings of emptiness that reflect the lack of a firm sense of identity. "I don't know who I am" is a plaint heard often from those with BPD. You can help your loved one establish a sense of selfhood. Understanding and dealing with this lack of identity is the subject of the next chapter.

CHAPTER 7

Identity: From Emptiness to Selfhood

Who are you? Most adults would identify themselves by their job, their connection to others (husband, wife, father, mother), their gender identification and sexual orientation, their interests, hobbies, what makes them laugh, what makes them cry. For the BP, many of these identity characteristics have not solidified. Moods may fluctuate like a mathematical sine wave, giddily oscillating above a steady demeanor before plunging below the level line into a deep bleakness. Borderline identity is like malleable, soft clay that can be sculpted into any shape, that can squeeze into any prefashioned mold, but without a model, it remains amorphous. The BP may sometimes appear like the skittish, hyperkinetic squirrel on the road that freezes, then starts to cross, then goes back, trying to decide which way to go.

This chapter examines how the BP may express struggles for a consistent identity and how you can help your loved one on that journey.

BPD and Identity

Establishing a sturdy sense of self is probably more difficult for most of us in the current cultural climate. Unlike in previous generations, there is greater geographic mobility in our society. Education and job demands interfere with the expectation of staying close to family. Americans are less likely than in the past to attend the same schools, churches, and social organizations as their parents. Relocations require adjustments to new friends, neighborhoods, and work parameters. With frequent moves, past stable anchors disappear. Social media (Facebook, Twitter, Instagram, computer dating, and so forth) reinforce barriers to intimacy. Ensuing isolation hinders the development of personal identity.

BPD is diagnosed three times more often in women than in men. In our culture female identity has probably experienced the most mutations, especially over the last fifty years. Women are expected to adapt more often from working life to motherhood, then back again. They may be expected to express ambition differently than men, as they advocate for equal pay and promotions. Feminism and societal changes call for more adjustments in a woman's self-perception. This may partly explain why striving for consistency in a world of constant change—a typical BPD struggle—may more often be identified in women.

Despite these cultural mutations, many people are able to grow up maintaining an environment of some consistency and predictability, developing a sturdy and enduring sense of self. They can preserve basic beliefs with minimal modification for new circumstances. But the BP, who has experienced less reliability in his existence and whose sense of identity is empty, must almost completely redesign his sense of self for a new environment.

For the BP, this adjustable identity is determined by what and who is around her and how those external forces make her feel at the moment. Contrary to Descartes's theory to prove existence, "I think, therefore I am," the BP's reassurance of her existence is more like, "Others act upon me, therefore I am."

In BPD, attitudes and temperament may transform in minutes. You may be bewildered by how rapidly and extremely the BP makes these changes. As he talks with you on his cell phone walking out of the office, he may reflect on how smart and accomplished he feels after receiving feedback on how well he handled the meeting. But when he gets to the car and sees he's locked his keys inside, he begins cursing and banging on the car, pulling his hair, and screaming about how stupid he is.

Or the BP feels pretty after compliments, but moments later, when the mirror reflects an emerging facial blemish, she feels ugly. When identity is focused primarily on body image, BPD may be accompanied by an eating disorder, such as anorexia nervosa, or by an obsession with what is overdetermined as a body flaw, such as a minor birthmark or nose shape, requiring immediate plastic surgery. (In medical nomenclature this is termed "body dysmorphic disorder.")

In your dealings with your loved one with BPD, you may encounter what seems like different personalities: the successful professional; the angry bitch; the demure lover; the aggressive, demanding friend. The BP may often remark that he feels he is playing a role or is "faking it." These identity changes are distinct from those found in the more severe and rare dissociative identity disorder (often referred to as "multiple personality").

Identity instability in BPD may appear in at least three different ways that I have labeled the "Chameleon," the "True Believer," and the "Distorter Absorber." When you recognize one of these patterns in a loved one, you can use some of the strategies examined below.

The Inconsistent Chameleon

In Woody Allen's 1983 film *Zelig,* the main character is able to assume the physical mannerisms, language, and personality of anyone around him. He takes on an Asian appearance when around Asians. He speaks French among the French. He uses appropriate jargon when confronted with a gaggle of psychiatrists. Emerging from a sense of internal hollowness and a desperate need to be liked, Zelig becomes a celebrity, nicknamed "the Chameleon Man." He becomes whomever those around him want him to be.

The Chameleon can be an exciting companion. In different situations she may be a reliable employee, a conscientious parent, and an alluring playmate. But if the various roles become confusing, or if the BP is uncertain of which persona to display, her anxiety may threaten the relationship.

> At college graduation Zoe was excited but surprised at how frightened she felt. She had already found a job as a receptionist in an obstetrician's office. She had located a small apartment nearby. She was making decisions alone, without her parents, without school counselors, without a boyfriend or roommate. But Zoe had expected to feel different as an adult—capable, confident, knowledgeable. And none of that was there. She needed to fake being "grown up."
>
> Gil first met Zoe at the gym. In pigtails and dressed in shorts, she looked to Gil like the all-American girl. He talked with her each time he spied her at the gym. She always seemed sweet and shy, playing with her pigtails while they talked, but after a brief time she would abruptly end the conversation and leave. Later Gil saw Zoe at a bar. At first he didn't recognize her. She was wearing a tight blouse unbuttoned provocatively and a short skirt. He had never seen her before with makeup, which was now heavily applied. She

was animated and gregarious. After talking a while he asked her out.

On their first dates she was the girl in the gym—pigtails, quiet, shy. On her birthday he decided to surprise her at work. Walking into the doctor's office, he told her coworker Annette that he just wanted to say hello to his girlfriend. "I'm right here, Gil," said the woman sitting next to Annette. He hadn't recognized her. Zoe was dressed in a conservative pantsuit with her bangs hanging over her eyes.

Gil's life became complicated when Zoe moved in with him. Sometimes she came home from work upset, telling him that Annette didn't like her and made fun of her. When Gil said he thought Annette was snobby and critical, Zoe began crying, insisting they were great friends. When she complained about a bartender making lewd comments when she was out with friends, she became angry when Gil asked what she'd been wearing. She would insist he was always blaming her when he questioned her role in situations. But she would defend the others involved if he was critical of them.

It seemed everyone knew a different Zoe. At work get-togethers the staff seemed to perceive her as very serious and hardworking, teasing that she needed to lighten up. Her girlfriends remarked on her drinking and life-of-the-party behavior. When she was with her parents, she was bouncy and agreeable, in her little-girl outfits and hairstyles. Gil lived with all of these Zoes.

The obstetrician for whom she worked asked her to assist him when he consulted at an abortion clinic. She readily agreed, telling Gil she wanted to stay busy and hoped to help women in need who were making difficult decisions.

Gil was stunned. "Zoe, our church is pro-life. You have always been so opposed to abortion. Remember when Marnie got pregnant and was going to terminate the pregnancy? You talked her out of it. You even went to the Lamaze classes with her. I don't understand why you want to do this now."

"You have never supported me. Every time I want to do something, you just criticize me," Zoe said, sobbing.

"I'm just saying, I don't understand how you can think one way one minute and then change your mind the next. It doesn't make sense."

"You never think I make sense. You think I'm just some silly little girl who needs her big strong man to take care of her," Zoe yelled. No longer crying, she was furious. "I don't need you to tell me what to think or how to feel! I don't need anyone. And I certainly don't need you."

Direct confrontation with the brittle Chameleon identity will usually prompt denial and anger. Any encounters of this sort should be front-loaded with support statements. Listen for "you don't understand" retorts signifying that the BP is not absorbing empathy communications and may be feeling misunderstood. Applying the SET mind-set is a helpful way to deal with strife in these situations.

Gil: "I agree, Zoe, it's great for you to want to do more to help people (SUPPORT), but I'm confused about your choice. You've always philosophically opposed abortion and have participated in all of our church's pro-life demonstrations."

Zoe: "Well, Dr. Samson said he could use help, and he knows how conscientious I am. He said he didn't think anyone else could do as good a job. So I said I would help."

Gil: "I know what you mean. When a person is flattering and needing you, it's hard to say no (EMPATHY). But I know you must have mixed feelings about this."

Zoe: [angry, not receiving the empathy and support messages] "You don't know how I feel. Why do you have to criticize everything I want to do?"

Gil: [sticking with support and empathy until she gets it] "I don't mean to criticize. I know you can do a lot for these women, and it would feel good to make such a contribution. Your compassion for others is one of the things I really love about you. But I also know about the things you did for Marnie and how you felt about that. And when we go to church...do you think your emotions might get kind of, well, confused?" (EMPATHY).

Zoe: "I don't know what you mean. And, besides, I can't disappoint Dr. Samson."

Gil: "Look, Zoe. You have sometimes expressed strong emotions in opposite ways. And I've also seen you get excited about things, and later feel disappointed or even guilty about it, and then get upset with yourself" (TRUTH).

Zoe: "So what do you want me to do?"

Gil: [avoiding the invitation to proclaim his prefer-ence, which would risk later blame] "Well, first I want you to know that I'll accept whatever you decide. It is certainly okay for us to have different viewpoints about things (SUPPORT). All I'm sug-gesting is that we both know that your feelings and attitudes about choices can change (TRUTH). And I think you should just take time to think over alternatives before making any big decision. Hell, that's good advice for anyone! I'm just concerned that this role could get really emotional and con-fusing for you. So if you want to think more about it, you could tell Dr. Samson you need a little

> more time to see what your schedule will allow. Or, if you want, we can discuss it some more or you could talk it over with a counselor. Whatever you decide will be okay with me, even if we agree to disagree."

Like Zelig, Zoe needs to be liked and accepted. Gil can help her, not by confronting and trying to disassemble her personality fragments, but by guiding her toward being more aware of how her feelings and attitudes change, and how others influence the development of contradictory emotions in her. This awareness can lead to her further self-exploration.

The True Believer

In his search for identification the BP is attracted to people and organizations that appear to offer controlled, disciplined direction and simplistic answers. He may cling to a group, religion, or belief system with a tenacity that becomes fanatical. He may reject friends who do not share his strong beliefs. He may abandon one commitment in order to join another. This pursuit to find himself may result in losing himself. For the partner, helping him find his way back can be daunting.

> After college Don found a lab job with a pharmaceutical corporation. He arrived early and stayed late, and he was precise, if not obsessive, about his assignments. He sometimes acknowledged others in the lab, but he mostly avoided contact. His boss, Pete, recognized Don's intelligence and dedication, and tried to mentor him. Don reluctantly accepted Pete's invitations for occasional dinners with his family, but he resisted Pete's suggestions for advancement opportunities.
>
> One day during his lunchtime routine of eating a sandwich by himself outside a few blocks from work, Don was

approached by a young woman. "Please excuse me, sir, but as I walked by, I saw your face and could tell you are troubled. You seem anxious. My name is Cindy," she said, smiling and offering her hand.

Don was dismayed. No one had ever approached him that way before, especially not a pretty girl. He reflexively offered his hand and told her his name. As they talked, Don felt more at ease. Cindy said she and her friends were having dinner later that evening and insisted Don come.

The dinner was in a hall downtown, where Cindy was waiting for him, along with about twenty other attendees. After dinner one of the men stood up and welcomed Don to the gathering. Then he gave a short lecture: "Everyone feels lonely sometimes. Everyone feels lost at times," he said. "But all of us here are learning how to find the real person inside. Our fellowship helps us achieve our maximum potential." The members referred to their organization as "Assemblage."

By the end of the evening Don felt different. He felt cared about. He felt he belonged. He enthusiastically pledged to continue attending meetings.

Over the following months Don returned to the hall daily. He participated in Assemblage's charitable activities, helped with the organization's fund-raising, and began donating a sizable portion of his paycheck.

At work Don became more reclusive. He no longer bothered to respond to colleagues' morning greetings. He brusquely refused Pete's invitations. He was now coming in late and leaving early. His production was becoming sloppy and sometimes incomplete. Finally, Pete confronted the significant changes in his behavior. Don explained that he'd become involved in the self-growth program Assemblage. "I am working with real friends to achieve my maximum potential," he said.

Pete first laughed, then became upset. "Don't be a fool!" he shrieked. "Everyone knows that place is a cult. You need to get out of there."

Don was enraged. "You have no right to tell me what to do. I shouldn't be around toxic people like you. I really don't belong here." He hesitated for a moment and then said, "I quit!" as he stormed out.

The True Believer is searching to fill an emptiness. She is most attracted to a construct that offers black-and-white filler for what she feels is missing. She searches for Oz, where a wizard will supply courage, a brain, a heart, or whatever she feels is lacking and whatever will provide a strict structure for contentment.

The True Believer is attracted to a closed system that offers acceptance into a special group that excludes outsiders. You may be among those excluded. To maintain the relationship, you must accept that the BP may be unable to readily relinquish a toxic belief system without someone or something else to hold on to. Healthier interests might include joining sports teams or special-interest clubs, or developing hobbies. You may be able to join in on some of these new activities. But your major goal is to avoid being totally shut out of your relationship, even if the BP continues contact with the exclusionary, cultish group.

With this goal in mind, Pete could reframe the entire interaction with Don:

Pete: "Don, I'm concerned about you (SUPPORT). You seem so unfriendly and annoyed, like you don't want to be here. Your work hasn't been up to your normal standards. You are usually more reliable and dedicated. This just isn't like you."

Don: "I've been involved in the group Assemblage."

Pete: "I've heard of Assemblage. It seems to be taking up all your time. What do you do there?"

Don: "Lots of things. We do charitable work. We have meetings where we help each other. Most people just don't understand."

Pete: "You may be right. But, you know, a lot of people don't understand chemistry, either, and I'm still friends with them. We just talk about other stuff. Seriously, I just want you to know that I care about you and am worried (SUPPORT). You seem to have shut out the rest of the world."

Don: "Assemblage provides me with what I need. It helps me achieve my maximal potential. The rest of the world only gets in the way."

Pete: "You know, some people think Assemblage is a cult that preys on people's insecurities. They say that they pressure people to turn away from friends and family, and commit a lot of money to the group" (TRUTH).

Don: "That's just part of the bullshit rumors people spread."

Pete: "Don, I'm not trying to tell you what to do. I'm concerned about you. I don't want to lose your friendship and the great things we accomplish at work (SUPPORT). It must feel really good to be part of a group, to feel you belong (EMPATHY). That's how I feel with my buddies in my soccer league. But there are people who have been in Assemblage and then left. And if what they say is true, it can be harmful. Being accepted and part of something bigger can be wonderful, but not if you lose the right to think for yourself. Not if you're told how to think or who it's okay to be with. Not if you're giving your savings away, yourself away. If you are really growing as a person, then it should be possible to have room for other people and things in your life (TRUTH). I just don't want to lose the Don I know and work with (SUPPORT). I hope you'll leave room in your life for the rest of us. Will you at least think about what I'm saying?"

Don: "I'll think about it."

Over the next few weeks, although Don still rejected Pete's invitations to dinner with his family, he did agree to go to lunch with Pete one day, where Pete said he'd read some of the Assemblage brochures Don had given him. Afterward, although Pete was still skeptical about the group, he told Don that he contributed to some of the same charities the group did. Finding common ground, they were able to maintain their relationship.

A True Believer feels she has found the answer to her life's insecurities in a new group or program. The need to belong can be overpowering. This need requires conformity and rejection of contradictory points of view. You must question her beliefs carefully. You can express empathy by acknowledging how important the group is to her, but you should never force her to feel like she must choose between you and the affiliation. Find a way to compromise so that she can continue engaging in the program while still maintaining her connection with you. Gradually, she may be able to detach from the organization.

The Distorter Absorber

Sometimes the BP, while groping for a sense of purpose and identity, develops a false impression of self. He may absorb a certain role to which he clings, despite contradictions. He may, for example, insist he's the best tennis player at his club, yet he doesn't qualify for the championship matches each year because of his sore back, twisted knee, disinterest, what have you. To maintain the self-perception, the Distorter Absorber may misrepresent the reality of a situation or the behaviors of others.

There may be a history of frequent job changes, several marriages and divorces. Explanations may be elaborate but similar: Each boss was "mean." Every coworker was "gossipy." Each spouse was "abusive." Your loved one is never at fault. Her characterizations may vary significantly from your experience of the person or situation. You may have known the boss, coworker, ex-spouse, or friend and found them not as she described them.

The distortion may progress to overt lying in order to preserve the self-perception. Conscious lying can even mutate into a break with reality, actually believing the untruth to be factual. At times the BP may become temporarily psychotic with hallucinations and delusions.

In this search for identity the BP presents you with a different dilemma: Is he exaggerating? Is he lying? Has he fabricated a belief system that is not real? Your goal then is to help bring the BP back to a reality assessment that is more truthful and establish communication that you understand and can trust.

Cory and Ann began working as paralegals in the law office at around the same time. Ann's family lived an hour away, but Cory had no contacts in town. Cory insisted that she and Ann were going to be best friends, and they spent a lot of time together. However, Cory seemed hurt whenever Ann made plans without her, especially when Ann spent weekends with her family.

When Ann confronted Cory's reluctance to be around her family, Cory confessed that the closeness of Ann's family made her melancholy about her own. Cory was an only child. Her mother had died years before. She told Ann she was very close to her father, but he worked for a government agency and traveled most the time. They rarely spent time together.

Ann was sympathetic. When Ann inquired more about her father, Cory would reply that his high-security job didn't allow for sharing details, but he would sometimes call to tell Cory he was swooping into town for a day or would send her a ticket to join him somewhere for a day. It all sounded quite romantic and exciting to Ann, who enjoyed hearing about their past adventures.

One morning Cory arrived at work in tears. She told Ann her father had a possibly cancerous lesion and was undergoing tests. Wanting to console her friend, Ann brought over dinner that night and then began spending more evenings with Cory to help her through this difficult time.

Once Cory seemed more settled, Ann came over less often. That's when Cory told her the doctors had diagnosed cancer and would start treatment. Worried when Cory related that she wasn't sleeping and had no appetite, Ann resumed regular visits, and so a pattern emerged: every time it seemed like the situation improved, Ann would pull back, then Cory would call soon after, relating worse news.

A few months later Cory did not appear at work one morning. When Cory didn't answer Ann's phone calls, she went over to Cory's house; through inconsolable tears, she told Ann her father had died.

For several weeks Ann spent as much time as possible with her friend. Cory told Ann that she was the only person left in the world who meant anything to her, that she didn't know what she would do without her. Ann's sense of obligation increased as she became more worried about Cory's health.

But two months later Ann was stunned to receive a call from Henry Jasper, Cory's father. "Cory told me you're a good friend, and I'm worried about her," he said. Henry explained that Cory had been distant for several years, ever since he'd remarried. She wouldn't visit them, though he lived only fifty miles away. Now she wasn't even returning his phone calls. Ann had many questions for Henry, which he politely answered. Yes, he worked for the government—the city government, in the courthouse. No, he didn't travel for his job. And his health was fine.

"How could you do this?" Ann screamed at Cory. "You made me believe you were helpless and grieving. I was doing everything I could to try to help with your tragic loss. And then it turns out to be nothing but lies. I will never trust you again!"

"Please, Ann," Cory pleaded, in tears. "I never meant for it to go this far. You're my only friend. When I was sick with the flu, you came over with soup and were so thoughtful. I never felt so cared about. I wanted to have that all the time. I wanted to be the person you'd want to be around all the time. And I guess that person would be someone who needed you to take care of her.

"My dad really did have a skin lesion that turned out to be benign. When I saw how concerned you were, I guess I needed to keep it going. The story kept growing, and after a while I think I really began to believe it. And since my dad and I really aren't in contact anymore, it feels in a way like I did lose him. Ann, we're such good friends. I don't want to lose you, too."

Ann was perplexed. She really did enjoy their friendship before the fiasco about Henry. She recognized that she had played an inadvertent role in Cory's fantasy by expressing fascination with her fabricated adventures, and she also realized that she'd liked playing the rescuer and so had unintentionally encouraged Cory's dependency.

Ann considered ending the friendship, but she ultimately decided to try to maintain the original closeness she'd developed with Cory. To do this, though, she would have to establish clear boundaries of what was acceptable. She would need to be aware of her own tendency to be a caretaker, and Cory would have to work to rebuild Ann's trust.

Ann: "Cory, we've been close friends for quite a while, and you know how much I care about you (SUPPORT). It's also obvious that you have gone through some difficult times lately, especially with your family (EMPATHY). But the elaborate charade you pulled on me—"

Cory: "I know..."

Ann: "It was unacceptable. It destroyed the trust between us. And it hurt your dad, too" (TRUTH).

Cory: "I know, I know. I'm sorry."

Ann: "If we're going to stay friends, I want to be friends with the real Cory. She is fun, caring, and reliable (SUPPORT). I don't want to be with the Cory you thought I wanted—the helpless, poor little Cory who has to stay helpless so I can take care of her. And I know I need to be aware of myself. I don't need to try to take care of everyone and make everyone happy. Let's just try to be ourselves. Our real selves" (TRUTH).

Distorted Misinterpretations

Part of the Distorted Absorber's typical profile is the tendency to misinterpret. Without a firm grasp of his identity and role in the larger world, he can question the motives of others, his lens for analyzing social situations can be cloudy, and he can frequently contend with anxious suspicions.

To help the BP better focus on the reality of things instead of his sometimes distorted perception of things, you can help him regulate misinterpretations. Downplay situations that he dramatizes; present other possibilities from a different, less threatening angle; explain that he may be blowing things out of proportion. A SET approach applies to the BP's misinterpretations as readily as it applies to the BP's other challenges and can go a long way toward comforting his uneasiness.

Thursday after lunch at work Rebecca's office had a little get-together with cake and punch to celebrate a colleague's retirement. Josh was her cubicle mate and had grown quite fond of her over the past year that he'd worked there, noting how capable and witty and generous she was. He was the one who talked to her the most at work, the one who encouraged her to attend outings when the staff socialized together. He also noticed how anxious she became in group settings, where she seemed a bit lost and mostly kept to herself.

This afternoon was no exception. He saw her standing in a corner of the break room, skeptically squinting over the rim of her cup at a huddle of coworkers who were looking around the room and laughing. When he went up to her, she didn't try to hide her suspicion that they were laughing at her.

"I understand you think the other people in the office are talking about you," Josh said, "and that must make you feel really uncomfortable (EMPATHY). Sometimes when I'm at a party or some gathering, I'll see unfamiliar people whispering to each other and looking in my direction, and I'll think for a moment, 'They're talking about me.' And then I have to tell myself, 'They don't know me, why would they bother babbling about me?' And then I think, 'Even if they were mocking me, what do I care, I don't know them!' We're in a really busy office. I doubt anybody has much time to worry about anyone else. And even if some were gossiping, who cares? They're not that important to you anyway" (TRUTH).

Josh regulated Rebecca's likely misinterpretation by refocusing her distorted lens in a way that seemed casual and conversational as opposed to serious and confrontational. He quelled her anxiety by reassuring her that she wasn't alone in her insecurity and, in the process, was able to deflate her growing distortion.

Psychotic Distortions

Sometimes, however, the BP's distortions meld into transitory frank delusions, characterizing what is termed "brief psychotic episodes." These breaks with reality may take the form of auditory or visual hallucinations, paranoid delusions, or dissociative periods in which the BP is unaware of his activities for periods of time. These episodes usually occur at times of extreme stress. As suddenly as the episode materializes, it may just as abruptly disappear, confounding those around him.

Lance was worried about Felix. They were both feeling the pressure of college finals, yes, but Felix's girlfriend had broken up with him a few days before, and Felix was acting strange. He had always been a little hard to get along with— very moody with a bit of a temper. But this was different. He was muttering to himself. Then he became more agitated, yelling incoherently. Lance kept asking him what was wrong, but Felix would only say something about "voices" telling him he was "empty." He began thrashing about the dorm room, knocking over the lamp and books on his desk.

"Don't let them make me kill myself," Felix pleaded, grabbing Lance's arm. Frightened, Lance tried to calm Felix, who seemed distracted and unable to hear him as he paced around the room. Lance called 911, and Felix was taken to the emergency room.

The psychiatrist in the ER told Lance that they'd ruled out drug use and other causes, that Felix was suffering from paranoid schizophrenia. The doctor said they would keep Felix in the psychiatric unit for the next several days while they medicated him. He told Lance that the hospital would call Felix's family to help with his withdrawal from college and to take him home and arrange for further intensive treatment.

However, the next morning when Lance returned with clothes for him, Felix appeared back to normal. He said he had vague memories of being upset the previous day and coming to the hospital, but after sleeping well, he felt fine and was waiting for the doctor to discharge him. "They've been treating me pretty good," he exclaimed. "The nurses are nice. The food is terrible. And they gave me some drug yesterday that made me feel goofy. So I refused it this morning." Just then the psychiatrist arrived, and Lance left for the waiting room.

A short time later Felix walked out, the doctor behind him. "Let's go," Felix announced. Lance looked at the doctor, who shrugged. On the way home Felix explained that the doctor had apologized to him. "He thought I was schizophrenic, of all things," Felix said. He continued explaining that the doctor called it "a brief psychotic incident, or something like that," related to stress. "He told me to get plenty of sleep and take it easy, whatever that means."

Lance just witnessed what a temporary break from reality looks like in a Distorted Absorber BP, and he did the right thing by calling for professional help. Under stress the BP's grasp of reality can completely unravel. At such times trying to convince her that the hallucinations aren't real won't help and can actually cause her to be more combative. Calling for medical help is necessary.

The Quest for Authenticity

The BP is compelled to take on a role that feels authentic. The role defines who he is and fills a void. He can then establish some semblance of an identity. But this identity is not one established over time, continuously molded from childhood through adolescence into adulthood. It is more fragile, less solid. If it falters, emptiness returns. To maintain it, the BP may try to embellish it. But you should recognize that this fabricated role and the manipulations to sustain it may sometimes be developed to provide what the BP thinks you require. You must examine how you may contribute to this process.

You can also deal with his insecurities by emphasizing your caring for him as unconditional. Although you applaud his successes and share his frustrations, none of these alter your feelings toward him. It may help to share some of your own flaws and disappointments, and your conviction that, despite these, he is still accepting of you, as you are of him. Help the BP to accept himself as someone with virtues and flaws, and to recognize your commitment to him.

Your loved one can fill some of the emptiness that partially defines BPD by developing a dependable sense of who he is, what his values are, and the ability to understand his world, even with its contradictions. As you and your loved one separate the falsehood from reality, you can start over together again with a more consistent, trusting relationship.

Action Steps

You can help your loved one attain a sturdier sense of self by displaying your own commitment and consistency. As you understand the reasons for identity shifting, you can discover how best to cope with it.

Be accepting, be consistent, be there.

The BP is struggling with defining who she is. She needs to feel accepted and cared for. It is important for her to know that you are understanding and supportive of this quest to establish who she is. In this chapter's examples it was important for Gil to assure Zoe that he was accepting of whatever work decisions she made; and Pete made clear to Don that he didn't want to be omitted from his life, but hoped to maintain a connection with him.

Encourage follow-through.

The Chameleon BP may jump from project to project, never fully finishing the activity. Encouraging him to complete activities helps develop consistency and self-esteem. Urge him to carry out the assignment. Try to dissuade him from prematurely dropping out of the class or quitting the job.

Participate in healthy activities together.

Exercise, attend lectures, and go to movies and art shows with your loved one to help her establish an assortment of likes and dislikes that will further define her sense of self.

Be part of a team.

The True Believer BP may isolate himself. Opening up his world can be liberating. To expose him to people outside his circle, join a bowling league or softball team together, take him to your church service, or invite him to your barbecue.

Twelve-step programs conduct an "intervention," which usually involves a group of people confronting an addict who denies his issues. In a similar way having a team of friends and family can be useful in confronting the True Believer whose behavior with his chosen group is becoming more destructive. Truth expressed by a group of caring others is harder to deny.

Avoid an ultimatum.

Forcing a choice may result in getting shut out. Don't make abrupt demands like, "If you really love me, you'll give up this organization" or "You have to choose—either me or your group."

Instead, try to gradually ease into her routine. You can express your disapproval of the activity, but concede your acceptance of her participation. Don't prolong a repetitive debate.

Recall from the scenario above that only after Pete expressed empathy for Don's involvement in his chosen group and emphasized missing time with him were they able to maintain their friendship.

Don't argue with psychosis.

If there is complete dissociation of identity, severe paranoia, or an outright break with reality, focus on trying to keep the BP calm. Don't argue that his hallucinations aren't real. Get medical help.

Acknowledge your own mistakes.

You may sometimes become frustrated and lose patience with your loved one. You may lose your temper. You may try to calm her down by offering unrealistic solutions. You may pretend to agree, then later be exposed. If you genuinely contributed to the problem, admit it. In such situations SET endorses a supportive statement of caring, empathetic recognition of the hurt you inflicted, and truthful acceptance of your responsibility.

Don't make all the decisions.

If you are the one who seems to be always choosing the activity, acknowledge that to your loved one. His consent may be more a need to maintain a passive, noncontentious role with you than an affirmation of constant agreement. Seek his input more actively. What movie, what restaurant, which friends, what does he want to do tonight? Don't attempt to fill his emptiness by taking over for him. Instead, encourage him to make decisions, to think about what he wants and doesn't want.

If your anger or disappointment frightens the BP, he may mislead you in order to avoid your upset. If you lost your temper, apologize and emphasize that even if you disagree or are frustrated, being truthful with each other is what is most important for your relationship.

Maintaining any relationship is hard work. When the person important to you lacks a sturdy sense of self, it is more challenging. When there are abrupt changes in that person's behavior, it can be frightening. You may be tempted to confront constantly changing and contradictory behaviors. You may try to fill the missing sense of self by leading the BP to your way of thinking and feeling. It is best to help the BP find her own way—to allow her to adapt to her own mistakes and successes. Focusing on trust in the relationship is paramount. And trust can only be established where truth can be accepted.

This need to fill that emptiness can be overwhelming for the BP at times. At such a point she may give up and feel she will always be an unhappy victim. This is what we'll explore in the next chapter.

CHAPTER 8

Victimization

The BP often sees himself as a victim. Disappointments, abuses, betrayals may all lead to disillusionment and certainty that he will never achieve contentment. There may arise a sense of guilt, a feeling that mistreatment is deserved. The BP may then assume hopelessness, that he can never be happy, that he deserves his miserable fate. And he is therefore justified in abandoning any attempts to change and get better. The victim role can also validate his borderline behaviors and project blame onto others. "The reason I can't stop using is because you keep hurting me." "Alcohol is the only thing I have in my life that makes me feel better." "After all I've done for you, this is all I get back."

Thus, sometimes it is your loved one who feels guilt-ridden and self-blaming, who feels punished. But at other times you may feel you are the one being pummeled, as the perpetrator of the BP's unhappiness. If you become the recipient of projected guilt, it becomes unclear who is really the victim and who is punishing whom. The BP insists she is suffering because you cause her misery or because you are unable to relieve it. But you may come to feel that you are the battered one, continuously accused of causing her unhappiness and berated for your impotence in relieving it. The victim thus victimizes you by withholding any validation of your attempts to help.

This chapter addresses how the victimization role emerges in BPD and the ways you can respond. It is important to recognize how easy it is to get entangled in this victimization role. You may feel pulled into sharing the sense of hopelessness, or you may feel a responsibility to magically solve the problem and rescue the relationship. You want to use the techniques described to avoid reinforcing your loved one's feelings of hopelessness, as well as to avoid feeling that you must either be his hero or the perpetrator of his unhappiness.

The Feeling-Bad-About-Feeling-Bad Trap

The negative self-image of BPD may reinforce negativity. Your loved one may pile on self-criticism. She may cut on herself when she gets anxious. Then she may get angry at herself for losing control. Then she may feel even more depressed over the new scar. All of this then reinforces her sense of helplessness.

But you also may become ensnared in a looping self-condemnation. You may sometimes feel responsible for the BP's unhappiness. You may blame yourself for her distress. Later, you may become frustrated that your attempts to help are fruitless or even condemned for worsening the situation. You may stack up more of your own self-criticism—for taking on too much responsibility, for losing your temper, for feeling incapable of helping… for feeling bad about feeling bad. While trying to help your loved one monitor this overload of self-punishment, make sure you are not infected. Take a step back to be sure you are not stacking up self-criticism. Be supportive, empathetic, and truthful to yourself, too.

> After her job was terminated, thirty-year-old Audrey had to move out of her apartment and back in with her mother,

Martha. Martha's mothering style in raising Audrey mostly operated by instilling guilt and complaining about her life. "How do you have the nerve to ask me for the car when you know how hard it is for me to support both of us?" "Did you want me to have a heart attack worrying about you when you came in after curfew?" "You must have done something wrong to make your girlfriends mad at you!" "Do you know how humiliating it is for me to go clothes shopping with you after you've gained all that weight?"

When Audrey would share a frustration in her life with her mother, Martha would often respond by relating how her own worries were much worse. Frequently, Martha would divert the focus back on herself: "I must be a really terrible mother that somehow you just can't stay on your diet." Audrey usually quietly absorbed these reflections and withdrew into a puddle of self-criticism.

One evening while Audrey was loading the dishwasher, Martha peered over her shoulder. "I've told you this a million times," Martha shrieked. "You know I'm on a blood thinner. The forks and knives need to face down, not up. I could cut myself and bleed to death right here before you could even call for help. I guess you think that's what I deserve. You've got me so upset now, I think I'm going to faint."

This time Audrey couldn't take it. She screamed at her mother for the first time in years. "Damn it, Mother! All you ever do is find more things to feel sorry for yourself about! I can't take this. You don't like the way I load the dishwasher? You load the fucking dishwasher!" Audrey slammed a cup in the sink, breaking it as she flew out of the kitchen. Martha sunk to the floor crying.

From her room Audrey could hear her mother wailing in the kitchen, and she began to feel guilty. She started to go to Martha to apologize and console her, but she decided to first call her best friend, Vicky, to talk it over. As she related the story, Vicky started laughing.

"Vicky, why are you laughing?" Audrey asked. "This isn't funny."

"I'm sorry," Vicky replied. "I'm not laughing at you. I'm just amused by the craziness of the whole scene. Your mom is criticizing how you load a damned dishwasher and accused you of trying to kill her through bleeding fingers, and all hell breaks loose. That could be like, I don't know, a *Golden Girls* episode or something."

"Yeah, but now she's on the kitchen floor crying her eyes out, and I feel terrible."

"Why?" Vicky asked.

"Well, she's my mother and—"

"But she kind of brings this on herself, don't you think? I mean, your mother has always done this poor-me, martyr shtick."

"Yeah, but I still think I should feel bad about it. I mean, I should feel more guilty or something."

"So," said Vicky, "you feel bad because you *don't* feel bad?"

"No! Actually, I think I feel bad *because* I feel bad. I really shouldn't feel guilty at all. Mom has been pulling this stuff on me my whole life. It's stupid for me to feel bad about it."

"Yes," affirmed Vicky. "But don't start beating yourself up for that. 'Cause then you'll feel bad about feeling bad about feeling bad!"

After the conversation Audrey felt less oppressed and more in control. She felt she understood her mother better. She returned to the kitchen, where her mother was still sitting.

"I'm sorry, Mom. I shouldn't have yelled at you," Audrey said, helping her mother stand up.

"I should say so. And after all I've tried to do for you, even with my medical problems," retorted Martha.

Audrey smiled to herself, more mindful of Martha's obvious attempts at inducing guilt with her martyrdom. "I know, Mom. Surely, it's been a strain on you having me move back here. I hate to put an extra burden on you. It would be hard on anyone making adjustments (EMPATHY). You're my mother and I will always love you and do appreciate your help (SUPPORT). It's your house and you have a way of doing things. I'll try to conform to your ways while I'm here. And if I get this job I've been interviewing for, I'll find my own place right away."

"Well," said Martha, "there's really no hurry. I like having you here. You can stay as long as you like."

"Thank you, Mom. I know I can always depend on you (SUPPORT, though *not* TRUTH). But we both have our own styles of how we like to do things. It's probably just better for us to have our separate spaces" (TRUTH).

In most cases when a victimization role is firmly embedded, it is difficult to change it by attacking the behavior. Without insight into her hopeless attitude, the BP has no motivation to change. Your attempts to contradict her need to pile on, to persist in being self-critical, to continue to feel bad about feeling bad may just make her more frustrated.

Your goal then becomes continuing the relationship at a level that does not hurt you. It is necessary for you to gain perspective, to not readily accept projected blame. It helps to understand that this is how the BP protects herself from the emotional pain that would accompany questioning her way of handling conflicts. To avoid responsibility, she must view herself as the vulnerable one, the one who is victimized, and therefore the one who has no responsibility for the distressful encounters.

Understanding this need to adhere to the victimization role makes it easier to shield yourself from absorbing projections of blame or guilt. Even when you do regret some of your responses, it is okay to not pile on more feeling bad about your reaction. And it is okay to not feel bad when you may feel glad, or relieved, when you can emotionally distance yourself from the BP. There are times when the BP may need to continue feeling bad about feeling bad. But you don't have to.

Confronting the Victimization Role

Over time you can eventually confront and soften victimization. Premature, direct challenge—"It's not that bad"; "You're just feeling sorry for yourself"—won't be helpful. The BP often feels that his hurtful experiences are unique and cannot be understood by others. He feels past failures give him the right (and excuse) to give up. He may wallow in his helplessness. You can empathetically acknowledge your understanding of why the BP feels hopeless after his damaging traumas. You can be supportive by reminding him that he has somehow been strong enough to endure the harm. And you can truthfully point out that, despite the hurt, he is maintaining his job, raising his kids, managing his life—although he might feel that he should give up, he hasn't.

Sometimes revealing your own vulnerability can help your loved one be more open about her disappointments. Sharing should not be presented as a comparison ("Oh, yeah, that happened to me, too"). That only challenges the BP's insistence on the uniqueness of her situation. Instead, you are trying to demonstrate that you, and others, can understand the wish to stop trying. If your loved one can talk more openly about her pain, then you can help her gain perspective. When she's more trusting, she'll be more responsive to your attempts to help her see differences between past frustrations and her current situation.

> Ethan was immediately fascinated by Roz. He found her Goth appearance and dark humor intriguing. But Roz put up barriers. She questioned his attention. She asked why he wanted to spend time with her. She had nothing to give. She told him that life had given her a raw deal from the start. For

a while she thought she could turn it around, but, well, it turned out she couldn't. And that was that.

Still, Ethan persisted. She finally consented to go out with him. But the going was rough. When he complimented her appearance, she said he was just trying to get laid. When he playfully teased her, she claimed he was making fun of her.

"Why do you make it so hard for me to be with you?" he asked her.

"Why do you even want to be with me? You don't know me," she replied.

"Well, that's the point—to get to know you."

"Believe me, you don't want to get involved with me," Roz said. "Ethan, you're a nice guy. But relationships don't work for me. Run along and find someone who will really care."

Other men usually gave up at this point. But Ethan liked Roz and wasn't ready to let her go. He figured that the dark shroud of mystery she hid behind concealed a painful past she wasn't open to talking about. So he told her about his life, his parents' painful divorce, the bullying at school, the failure of his marriage. He told her how hard it was for him to deal with these setbacks and how they still affected him.

Roz then felt comfortable enough to tell him about Beau. He had been persistent too. Beau had also wanted to get to know her. He could make her feel better. Heroin. When they used, he was mellow and relaxed. But other times he was violent and abusive. She could cover over the bruises, but when he broke her arm, they had to go to the emergency room.

When Ethan said Beau was a detestable person, Roz protested, "It was always my fault. I knew how to get to him."

She became angry when Ethan insisted that her behavior could never justify physical abuse. "You don't understand," she said. "I killed him!"

Roz explained that after their last violent exchange, she threw the needle they'd been sharing at him and screamed, "Go get high, junkie. That's all you're good for!" and had locked herself in the bathroom, where she fell asleep. The next morning she found him on the back porch, dead of an overdose.

"I hated that prick," she said, sobbing. "I was glad he was out of my life. Isn't that horrible? I feel terrible."

"He beat you. He was a miserable, sad person," Ethan said. "Of course you were relieved he was gone" (EMPATHY).

"I'm disgusting," Roz continued. "What kind of awful person is glad a human being is dead?"

"Roz, I care for you. Let me be in your life and try to help. I don't believe you are this bad person you think you are (SUPPORT). You are so hard on yourself! You seem to put yourself in this kind of box in which no matter what you do, you see yourself as a bad person. If you truly missed someone who so horribly treated you, you would be kind of a helpless masochist who expects to continue to be abused. But if you feel gratified that this man killed himself, well, that makes you a triumphant sadist. So you can beat yourself up either way: you can feel depressed about being so defective that you deserve to be abused; or you can feel guilty about feeling relieved that you're no longer being mistreated."

For the victimized BP, it's her against the cruel world. And the world won. Game over. But with patience and perseverance, you can penetrate that barrier of helplessness. Although she feels weak, you can point out the strength she must possess in order to have survived the troubles. You can help her understand how she anticipates losing the fight, even when there is no opponent. You may be able to help her expand a perspective that goes beyond her own trials to recognize how others contend in the world. This gains a broader perspective for how she can survive in an environment that is not as hostile as she might think. And she can begin to accept that past frustrations don't have to dictate future disappointment.

Action Steps

Interacting with BPD victimization requires walking a very narrow path. You need to empathize with your loved one's pain and express your understanding of his feelings of hopelessness. Yet, you are not collaborating with his insistence that he is helpless. It is important to balance truth with support and empathy.

Appreciate the positive.

Focus on the progress the BP has made *despite* her handicaps. You can agree that she has been victimized, yet you can also commend the strength she must possess in order to have endured.

Pointing out the positive might sound like this: "A lot of other people who have experienced what you've gone through would be in a hospital or jail or dead by now. You must be a pretty tough cookie to have survived it all." Or, "Let's face it. You've had some bad breaks. But I really admire the fact that despite all that, you've still been able to accomplish so much."

Emphasize that just surviving trauma is the first triumph. Further progress is even more admirable and contradicts the position that the BP is a hopeless victim.

Help the BP gain perspective.

The sensation of passing time for the BP is disproportionate. The future that is tomorrow may seem like years away. And short bursts of the past may continue to inhabit major chunks of the present. The past traumas that instigate the victimization role of BPD may have occurred many years ago. Yet these injuries may continue to feel overwhelming and influence present experience. Helping your loved one put past disappointments within the context of a lifetime can be extremely productive.

You don't have to insist that past hurts should be forgotten or don't affect current feelings. Accepting the past doesn't imply forgiveness or validation. But it is the past. After establishment of support and empathy comes the truth that yes, indeed, your loved one has experienced awful situations, mistreatment, and plain bad luck. The unfairness of life can be a bitter truth. And many others have also suffered shattering traumas, some even worse. But though the past can cripple, the present can begin healing, and the future may lead to recovery.

Sometimes restating the circumstances in a different context helps the BP keep them in proportion. Contextualizing may also help you when you feel frustrated and sometimes even angry hearing the same complaints about the past repeated.

"When I hear your descriptions about how your parents favored your little brother, Jacob, and ignored you, it's easy to see how that could really affect you (EMPATHY). It almost sounds like a clichéd soap opera. Heck, a biblical soap opera: Jacob gets the blessings, and Esau, that's you, gets squat. He's the clever one, and you're just seen as the bumbling idiot. You told me about how they threw him this great big party for his graduation, but completely forgot your birthday. It's like one of those old teenage movies. If it weren't so hurtful, it's almost bizarrely funny. If you look at it from a distance, all you need is a laugh track and you have a TV sitcom. And still, considering all the things you have accomplished in your life, you've pretty much proved you're not that idiot (TRUTH). And I'm really proud to be someone who is part of your life" (SUPPORT).

Empathize, but don't wallow.

It is important to communicate to the BP that you understand and accept that she has experienced overwhelming pain. You can agree that she has been treated unfairly. But don't leave it there. You can pledge your support in helping her deal with the situation. You can praise her courage for refusing to give up. But don't collude with her sense of hopelessness. Emphasize areas of success, such as sports, school, work, good friends. Point out outstanding qualities, like intelligence, sensitivity, friendliness, technical skills. Cite options for the future in which these qualities can lead to more satisfaction.

> "What happened to you back then is horrible and hard for me to even imagine (EMPATHY). But you know what? Tough shit! Life ain't fair, and it's too damned bad! You've obviously been strong enough to survive. So now we need to harness that strength and use it to continue your success from here on (TRUTH). And I want to be here to help" (SUPPORT).

Support, but don't try to be the hero or allow yourself to be the scapegoat.

Expect eventual improvement in BPD symptoms, but change comes slowly. Encountering a charming individual with an unhappy past can incite a wish to rescue. Avoid assuming the responsibility of the champion who will swoop in and make everything okay. The hero role can set you up for failure. Promises to fix it may not meet immediate expectations. You may then be the target for guilt projections: "You're just like everyone else who's let me down."

Assuming the hero role also reinforces the disparity in the relationship. The more you continue to be the rescuer, the more your loved one remains in the helpless victim role. As the inequality in the relationship continues, your character as admired hero may transform to that of resented, controlling oppressor.

Support and empathy for the situation can help your loved one feel understood. But don't expect immediate resolution of his victim role. Exhortations to "pull yourself up by the bootstraps" or "just stop feeling sorry for yourself" will be experienced more as further victimization than as helpful truth. Trust that emanates from support and empathy precedes considerations of the "now what do we do?" part of truth.

Newlywed Michael insisted to his bride, Sherry, that his job relocation would make her feel better. She would be away from her troublesome family, could quit her stressful job, and just focus on setting up their new house. But after a few months Sherry was more depressed than ever. Arranging the new house was overwhelming; she missed her mother, despite their constant fights; and Michael's new job kept him away for long hours.

"Michael, you promised me the move would be great," Sherry complained. "Well, maybe for you! You're at work all the time. You don't know what I'm going through at home. I hate this city. The neighbors are all snobs. Back home, at least, there were people to talk to. I should never have married you," she said, sobbing. "Let's face it. I should never have married anybody. I'm just a burden."

Michael was frustrated. He was tempted to defend himself and remind Sherry that she'd agreed with their decision. But that would reinforce Sherry's victim role ("You're right! It's my own damned fault!"). Instead, he took responsibility and confessed that he had unintentionally overglamorized the move. "I understand how difficult it must be for you to adjust to a new town, especially without having a job or any new friends yet" (EMPATHY). He pledged his support in helping Sherry integrate into the community.

"Now that I'm getting better situated at work," he said, "we'll spend more time together exploring the city. And, of course, we will plan visits home. We're starting a new chapter in both our lives. I know it's scary. But it can also be exciting. And we're doing it together" (TRUTH).

The BP's victimization is an attitude that has been marinating for many years. It can take a long while to adjust. You may become frustrated and impatient. You will need to resist being lured into the BP's pessimism and the feeling-bad-about-feeling-bad quagmire. But over time, by applying UP, you will see mellowing. With your understanding and perseverance, the relationship can proceed in a more equal partnership.

Victimization usually invokes passive acceptance of discouragement. The victim withdraws into darkened rooms of melancholy. But sometimes disappointment in oneself can turn into active and violent anger against the self. Self-destructiveness can be a terrifying aspect of BPD. In the next chapter we look at how to deal with it.

CHAPTER 9

Impulsive Self-Destructiveness

BPD is the only formal medical diagnosis that is partially defined by self-damaging impulsivity. Self-harm may take the form of self-mutilating behavior, like cutting or burning. You may discover your loved one drawn to substance abuse, gambling, overspending, binge eating or starving, promiscuity, reckless driving, and other compulsive, dangerous, and self-defeating behaviors. Self-destructiveness may even extend to suicidal threats or behaviors. These actions can confuse and alarm you.

It is important to understand that this self-harming tendency is a result of the BP's unhealthy attempts to cope with anxiety and emotional pain. Physical pain may distract the BP from internal agitation. It may serve to relieve a sense of numbness and retain a feeling of control over emotional and physical sensations. It may accommodate self-determined guilt and a need for self-punishment. Borderline self-destructiveness may also sometimes serve to punish you. This chapter focuses on how you can constructively respond to dilemmas like these:

- After arguments Arthur would often go on a bender. He would disappear for several days without contact, which he knew worried his wife. He would drink until passing out in his car or at a friend's house. When he returned home, he blamed his wife. "See what you made me do?"

- When angry at her boyfriend, Ruth would bombard him with detailed descriptions of her flirtations with other men. Some of the men she teased responded with menacing and sometimes aggressive reactions. Although she knew that this behavior threatened both her and her relationship, she blamed her boyfriend's frequent business trips for her dangerous behavior.

Encountering Self-Harm

Evidence of self-harm in someone you care about can alarm you, and that alarm can lead you to respond instinctively in the moment. Before discussing how to handle this situation, here's an example of how *not* to handle it.

Julio and Donna met on an online dating site and immediately felt connected. One evening, picking Donna up for their fourth date, Julio entered her apartment to find her very upset, standing in the entry hall, coat on, purse in hand, quietly sobbing. She answered his concerned questions, explaining she had had a big fight with her mother over the phone. She announced her intention of proceeding with their night out, despite her obvious distress. But Julio insisted that they should just relax at her place, order in dinner, and watch TV. As he helped her off with her coat, he was horrified to see that both arms were marked by multiple cuts, oozing blood.

Over her objections, he rushed her to the emergency room, where her wounds were closed and bandaged. Donna refused the psychiatric consult and signed papers to leave the hospital against medical advice. Julio's questions about her behavior were met with anger.

"I already told you about this," Donna responded to him. "It's my mother. She said she just called to say hi. But that's never it." Donna's voice grew louder as she went on. "She wanted me to give her more money again. She said she was going to be evicted. This bitch never did anything for me. She never gave me a damned thing. She always just took. She has always used me."

"That's horrible," Julio said.

"Ya think? So last night I said to her, 'No more, Mom. I can't bail you out anymore.' And she's screaming, saying I'm an ungrateful brat and that she hates me. She said she's sorry I was ever born. She said she will never talk to me again, then hung up. I've had it. I have no mother."

"But why did you cut yourself? It must have hurt."

"No, it doesn't hurt," Donna responded angrily. "It kind of helps. It calms me when I'm upset and angry."

"How can cutting on yourself help?" Julio asked. "That's just insane. I mean, I know what it's like. I've had to deal with crazy parents too. But I don't go around mutilating myself. You just have to get a hold of yourself and deal with it."

"Julio, don't tell me you know what it's like. You have no idea what it's like," Donna screamed. "And how dare you tell me to just 'deal with it'! Fuck you!"

"Well, same to you, Donna. Hey, I was just trying to help."

"Well, if this is what you call 'help'...just leave!" Donna shouted.

"Fine! That's exactly what I'll do," Julio retorted. "Man, you really had me fooled there for a while. I thought you were kind of normal. Your mother sure taught you well how to be a real bitch!"

Disarming Self-Harm

Julio's dismay at Donna's behavior sabotaged their relationship. His failure to fully understand Donna's anguish and his lack of empathy fueled her anger at him. Her furious responses signaled that she was not receiving what she needed most at that time: support and empathy. She was feeling judged and criticized, just like she's always felt with her mother.

Instead, insensitive to Donna's grief, Julio volleyed her hurt and fury with retaliatory spitefulness and tried to compare her frustration with his own. This tactic will be useless with a BP in the midst of emotional pain. You must try not to lose your temper in these heated moments. Attempting to understand your loved one's emotional experience is the first priority.

Julio: "I was so concerned last night (SUPPORT). I was afraid you were trying to kill yourself. You must have been feeling horrible to do that" (EMPATHY).

Donna: "Yes, that whole thing with my disgusting mother has been horrible. And, no, I wasn't trying to kill myself, for God's sake. If I really wanted to kill myself, I wouldn't do *that*."

Julio: "Well, what were you doing?"

Donna: "Look, just forget it."

Julio: "Donna, I really care about you. And I don't comprehend what happened. I've also noticed what looks like some old scars on your legs, too. I want to try to make sense of what you're going through" (SUPPORT).

Donna: [crying] "I don't know if I understand it. I just know that when I'm hurt or upset, I need to feel something physical in my body to calm the agitation."

Julio: "Doesn't it hurt?"

Donna: [not feeling the empathy] "No! And stop asking me that!"

Julio: "I just want a better understanding of the pain you must be experiencing (EMPATHY), so I can try to help" (SUPPORT).

Donna: "I don't know what you think you can do."

Julio: "Well, I can be here. You can call me when you're upset. We can look for other ways to relieve that tension (SUPPORT). I know we don't want to spend date nights at the emergency room. And I'm afraid you could make a mistake and cut deeper than you intended, and that could be dangerous" (TRUTH).

Donna: "Look, I know you're trying to help, but when stuff like this happens, I feel like I'm going to blow apart. I can't control it. I just need to do something to let it out."

Julio: "Well, I know one technique we could try when you're feeling that need for physical distraction."

Donna: "What's that?"

Julio: "I can hug and squeeze you as tight as I can."

Donna: "I'd like t o try that!"

You may be disturbed by some of the BP's self-defeating actions. Usually, he is not trying to kill himself, only to inflict pain. He may be ashamed to reveal such behavior and defensive about discussing it.

Exhibiting your willingness to understand, rather than judge, is important. Empathizing with the anguish that animates the behavior and emphasizing your caring for him can make him feel safe enough to examine it. Only then can the two of you together examine the truth of how this conduct is destructive to him and his relationship with you.

Facing the Destructive Adolescent

When the borderline individual is a child or young adult, the self-destructiveness that accompanies the disorder requires special considerations because the BP is not yet mature enough to take responsibility for her actions and to fully comprehend the consequences of those actions. This next scenario demonstrates how a fractured family can strive toward healing.

> After her parents' divorce when she was twelve, Missy went through a frightening transformation. Over the following three years she converted from the cute, sweet little girl with a ponytail to someone her mother, Dee, didn't recognize. Missy changed her appearance, wearing heavy makeup and sloppy clothes. She went from excelling in school to skipping classes. She rudely criticized her mother's cooking, clothing, and social life. She especially resented her mother's remarriage to Perry.
>
> Missy became more verbally offensive and physically aggressive. When angry, she ripped her favorite wall posters and smashed her valued CDs. She would leave the house for days to stay with her father, who reinforced some of her complaints about her mother. But when her father imposed limits, Missy threatened to run away and kill herself, and she ended up back at her mother's. She would leave the house at all hours and return home disheveled and glassy-eyed, dazed by drugs.
>
> Dee grounded Missy, but both knew the limits would be ignored. Dee announced curfews that she was unable to enforce. Dee demanded Missy see a counselor, but Missy refused to go. Perry tried to intervene, but Missy was

contemptuous. "You're not my father. I don't have to listen to you," she declared and walked away. Dee felt powerless. Missy was unbound.

When she came home with a blackened eye and a bloody nose, she confessed, after prodding, that a man she met had hit her. Missy told her parents they were at his apartment smoking hash when he showed her his gun. She dared him to play a kind of Russian roulette with it, but he got scared. "I got mad and started calling him names for chickening out," she said. "I deserved it. I was a real bitch."

When Dee and Perry tried to comfort her, she became angry and told them to stop trying to control her. When Missy announced she was going to stay with her father, Dee told her that her father had informed Dee that Missy could not stay with him anymore. If she showed up, he was not going to let her in. Missy was Dee's problem now, he had said. "Everybody would just be better off if I was dead," Missy exclaimed as she ran out of the house.

Dee called 911. She told the operator that her daughter had run off and was threatening suicide. She also asked that Missy be taken to the hospital when she was found, since Dee couldn't assure her safety at home. Dee recognized that her daughter needed to be contained in a safe environment until a plan could be devised.

Missy was admitted to an adolescent psychiatric unit. She hated the nurses and doctor, and was initially uncooperative, but when she soon realized her rebelliousness might prolong her stay, she settled down. For the first time controls were being instituted, and Missy could no longer avoid truth consequences for her behavior. The doctor suggested to Missy and the family that if self-destructive behavior continued, Missy could be transferred to a residential facility for adolescents, where she could expect to stay for several months.

Frightened by this proposal, Missy agreed—with her mother, father, and stepfather—to a behavioral contract that delineated specific behaviors that would allow her to transition out of the hospital and remain home. Positive rewards for healthy behavior replaced the need to find relief from self-destructive activity. As she gained more independence, Missy began to replace borderline rage and self-abuse with ordinary adolescent striving.

The adolescent bridge between the protected innocence of childhood and the mature freedom of self-understanding is often fragile. A self-destructive borderline teenager or young adult may not be able to healthily adapt to the evolving self-determination. In such situations parents or other caretakers must develop a consistent plan that all involved parties can support.

If parents are divorced, contentious feelings may persist. But for a program to work for their child, they must support each other. For the BP, consistency is often an absent quality and therefore must be prominent among those setting limits. Stepparents must be supportive of their spouses. All involved adults should put personal feelings aside to do what is best for the minor and make that concern the highest priority.

The BP who has not yet achieved independent living detests his dependence and resents those on whom he relies. He despises truth limitations and does not readily hear support and empathy sentiments. But don't be discouraged from continuing those comforting statements. At some point they can break through the resentful barriers.

Control what you can. Don't try to control what you can't. You may be able to maneuver the BP's activity, but you may not be able to influence her attitude about it. Limit setting must be enforceable. Demand nothing that cannot be practically carried out and that you are not willing to implement. Restrictions can also be balanced with benefits. For example, use of the car can be a reward for cooperation. Extra spending money and favored activities (like going to the skateboard park or attending a concert) can be granted when goals are met.

Action Steps

Because impulsive self-destructiveness can be dangerous, it is important to protect yourself, as well as your loved one. In case of an emergency you may need to respond immediately. In most interactions with your loved one support and empathy should always come before addressing truth issues. But in emergency situations truth may need to precede support and empathy. Being consistent and reliable when the BP's impulsive behavior may be inconsistent and unpredictable helps him establish his own boundaries and controls.

Keep the environment safe.

Minimize objects that could potentially be used in an impulsive, destructive gesture. Encourage the BP to discard bottles of medicine no longer used. Eliminate unnecessary razors or knives outside of kitchen use. Evaluate if a gun in the house is too readily accessible or even necessary.

Explore options to replace self-harm.

Intense, even exhausting physical exercise can discharge the tension or emotional numbness that generates the BP's need for self-destructive action. At times of anxiety, try going to the gym or taking a walk together. A stimulating hot tub soak or ice bath can relieve tension. Molding clay, vigorous painting or drawing, banging on a piano or other musical instrument can soothe. Some borderline impulses to self-harm may be alleviated by marking up arms or legs with red marker, simulating blood. Staying busy together distracts from self-destructive impulses. The ultimate goal is to help your loved one find other ways to relieve the internal tension.

Anticipate and prepare for potential acting out by predicting.

Recognizing in advance potential stressors for the BP can help you prepare her for the situation. Preparation includes predicting how the BP may be affected and how you can work together for a more satisfying response.

Chloe had been bulimic since early adolescence. Eating then throwing up made her feel in control and soothed her anxiety. With treatment, she was able to better control the eating disorder, but she intermittently continued the bulimia during times of stress.

Her husband, Clyde, knew her history and was supportive of her struggle. Both knew that a primary trigger for Chloe's anxiety was his widowed mother, who fortunately lived far away. A bitter, depressed woman, Clyde's mother was hypercritical of Chloe. Chloe and Clyde would come for annual family get-togethers, but Chloe's engagements with her mother-in-law sometimes led to her relapse. Before their upcoming visit Clyde tried to prepare both for the ordeal.

"Chloe, I really appreciate your willingness to come with me to visit my mom and the family. She can be so difficult! And it's excruciating for you (EMPATHY). We want to make sure she doesn't get to you like she did last year. I will do whatever I can to maintain the recovery you've worked so hard for (SUPPORT).

"I remember last time when you got upset, you left the party claiming a headache, snuck out some booze and cake, and then binged and purged. I want to prepare us this time for any repeat stress from Mom. So, first of all, I'm going to stay with you the whole time. If things get too distressing, I don't want you to go off alone again. Let's maybe have some kind of signal if you feel you need to get out. Cough twice if you know you have to leave. I'll say we're both recovering from a cold and need to go take our medicine. Then we'll take off and walk around for as long as you need, until you feel more in control."

Predicting triggers that may lead to a crisis should be done in a calm, nonjudgmental, matter-of-fact manner. In such a way you may ease some of the BP's anticipatory tension. Then, together, you can devise a plan to more adaptively respond.

Confirm that all involved parties are in agreement.

Confronting the BP's destructive behavior requires the cooperation of all engaged. Try not to allow someone else to sabotage a plan to limit self-harming action. Meet with others involved in the BP's life to ensure that everyone is on board with a consistent response to threatening behavior. They may include your spouse's mother, or your child's grandfather, a sympathetic friend or employer, or anyone who is unaware of the whole situation and could thus undermine your plan. Spouses may have to conceive of a compromise that they both agree they can support.

Be consistent.

Avoid promises you know you can't keep. Don't demand limitations you can't maintain. When you set boundaries that may be breached, have a plan ready to stick to those restrictions.

Darren repeatedly told his alcoholic brother, Jeff, that he would no longer lend him money and that Jeff needed to stick with a job and get help for his drinking and depression. But every few months Jeff would call again to say that he was about to be evicted or that people he owed money to were threatening him. He'd tell Darren that he was ready to just give up and drink himself to death. If Darren could just tide him over until he dried out and the new job started, he knew he could pull himself together.

Darren finally decided to discontinue the financial dependency. He told Jeff this would be the last time.

"I know I've said this before," Darren stated, "but this really will be the last time. I'm your brother and I love you (SUPPORT), but I fear that in a way my lending you money has interfered with your own need to adapt and be responsible for yourself (TRUTH). You're a proud man and have had to face some tough situations over the years (EMPATHY), but you need to get help to deal with your drinking and depression" (TRUTH).

"You're right," Jeff responded. "This is the last time I'll ask for anything, and I'm going to pay you back. I swear I'm going to pull myself together this time, and I can do it myself."

"You've said that before too, Jeff," Darren said. "And I know you mean it. But it hasn't worked that way, and we need to change things. First of all, I am going to send you another check. It's not a loan. It's a gift. Don't think you have to give back any of what I've sent you in the past. But this will really be the last time. I am going to research some alternatives. If you are needy in the future, I'll contribute some resources other than money."

When Jeff called back a few months later, Darren provided addresses and phone numbers for state assistance, mental health clinics, homeless shelters, food banks, and other relief benefits.

You may feel guilty when you decide to stringently sustain a limit that was previously more lax. Your loved one may feel abandoned and may try to amplify your guilt. In such situations it is important to explain why the change is really not so much a change, but a reinforcement of the original understanding. Use support and empathy in explaining why the truth adjustments are now necessary. It is best to make the adjustments gradual. Instead of ending financial assistance completely, taper it over time or provide enough for a reasonable time. Instead of demanding she leave the house immediately, discuss a future fixed date for leaving that you can stick to and that allows some time for her to adapt to the new agreement.

Don't accept projected blame.

You are not the reason the one you care about cut himself. You did not force him to go back to drinking. You aren't the one who made him have an affair. Empathy for the pain that he has endured does not lessen the truth that, ultimately, the BP must be responsible for the behavior.

You can be supportive without being swallowed up in guilt. Don't get caught in a distracting debate about your contribution to his actions. You can acknowledge your impact on how he feels, but focus on the truth of how, with your support, he can work on the problem.

When a threat of danger is imminent, concentrate on truth.

In most situations your pledge of support and demonstration of true empathy are the most important approaches to emphasize initially. When trust is established, the BP is more willing over time to consider painful truth options with you. But if you perceive that the risk of danger to the BP, or to you or others, may be imminent, you must invoke immediate, realistic truth measures to prevent harm.

Your loved one may vigorously object to your calling the doctor or hospital or police for assistance. She may try to minimize the amount of the overdose or the seriousness of the bleeding and insist you are overreacting. She may threaten to run away or terminate the relationship if you try to intercede. At these times you may be in a classic no-win predicament: if you accede to her demands and passively accept the potentially dangerous situation, you may be accused later of not caring enough to prevent her from harm; but if you deny her pleas to stand back and instead actively respond to her threats, you can be accused of disrespecting her and, again, of not caring.

It is better for the BP to understand that her self-destructive behavior is upsetting and is always to be taken seriously. In emergencies a rational truth response is necessary and is the message she needs to hear.

> "I know you're angry with me for calling 911, but I'm afraid. God, you must have been feeling horrible when you did this (EMPATHY). But you admitted you took the rest of the pills in that bottle, and I don't know how dangerous those drugs may be or how serious you are about this. But I am not going to stand around and let you risk killing yourself. Of course I'm going to call for help (TRUTH). You know how much I love you, and I am going to do whatever it takes to help you get better" (SUPPORT).

Suicidal threats and self-harming behaviors in someone you care about are frightening. Although you may feel powerless during crises, you are not. Staying calm during an acute event is difficult, but it heartens your loved one. You may be concerned that you don't know how to act or fearful that you may say something wrong. But your very presence is reassuring. Just being with him is a demonstration of your support when he is tormented and fearful that there is no hope. You may be puzzled when told how much you have helped. You may wonder what it is you said or did that was so comforting. It may only be that you just stayed there with him and persevered.

Understanding and perseverance over time will help you maintain the relationship. But there may come a time when you doubt your ability or willingness to persevere. In the concluding chapter we take a look at factors that encourage continuing to hang in there and circumstances that suggest letting go.

CHAPTER 10

When to Hold, When to Fold

Caring for someone with borderline personality disorder can be more demanding than you first imagined. All of the preceding chapters in this book have been devoted to helping you preserve your connection with this person. You have reviewed many examples of the common disruptive expressions of BPD. You have read about strategies to help deal with these behaviors. You have also learned that over time many of these behaviors gradually improve or resolve. Your interest in what has been presented here reflects your devotion to your loved one and your dedication to sustaining the relationship.

Every commitment to another requires some adjustments—to be less selfish, to be more sensitive, to curtail some other commitments, to compromise. But during turbulent encounters in any affiliation, there may be times when you ask yourself if it is worth it. If demands are too great and sacrifices too severe, you may consider withdrawing.

What it takes to sustain your relationship with someone with BPD is a very personal question. Just as everyone's tolerance of physical pain is different from one person to the next, so tolerance of how much emotional exertion people can make to maintain the connection varies. Obviously, if, after a considerable time, emotional anguish is too disabling and the likelihood of change in the BP is poor, you may need to give up the relationship. But before any intimate connection dissolves, you want to feel like you gave it your best shot. That includes couples or family therapy, counseling for yourself, and assuring your loved one is receiving the best help available. You also want to feel you have given the relationship adequate time to advance.

Reinforce Progress

The process of behavioral change for the BP often evolves in a kind of backward way—from after-the-fact recognition, to in-the-middle suspension, to preemptive control. Recognizing gradual adjustment and promoting its development enhances the advancement.

Afterward: "Whoops, I Did It Again!"

Change begins when the BP recognizes dysfunctional behavior *after* it happens. He starts to recognize triggers for his reactions and is motivated to avoid future missteps.

Lee had been frustrated at Mona's frequent calls to his workplace. After countless arguments Mona began to recognize that these calls were jeopardizing her husband's job and that they were a result of her own insecurities. She told Lee that she understood his concerns and agreed that her fears of being left were unjustified. She pledged to curtail the calls.

But after an especially stressful day she began calling again to complain about the day and demand reassurance, which made Lee increasingly angry. As she hung up after her latest, frustrating call, she recognized how maladaptive this behavior had become. She texted her husband, acknowledging and apologizing for her slip, and stating she would wait to talk to him when he came home.

That evening Lee avoided "I told you so" criticisms and instead made support responses about how proud he was of her for recognizing her old pattern and working to correct it.

Midway: "There I Go Again!"

Catching herself in the middle of a counterproductive action and stopping it is the next progression toward change.

In the midst of screaming at his girlfriend, Dina, for being a few minutes late, Hunter abruptly stopped. "I'm sorry," he said. "I've been trying to work on my temper, and I blew it again."

Dina avoided responding with angry criticism or "that's okay" acceptance, as she had done in the past. Instead, she emphasized empathy: "Wow!" she declared. "That was something—how you kept it together. I could tell you were angry with me, but you were able to manage it this time. You saw it and stopped it. You didn't lose control. I know how difficult that has been for you in the past. I'm really proud of you" (SUPPORT).

Preemption Before: "Let's Not Go There Again!"

Recognition of self-defeating behavior after it is expressed, then perceiving it while in the middle of conflict, and shutting it down before it progresses further are encouraging signs leading to change. Experiencing these revelations results in eventually diagnosing and anticipating stressors in advance, allowing the

BP to completely avoid succumbing to the old destructive reactions to the distress.

As you know, many BPD symptoms diminish over time. When you recognize a change in response, a different pattern, you want to reinforce it with the SET approach.

> "You know, in the old days, if we would have had this disagreement, you would have gotten furious and hung up on me. You might also have gone out and gotten drunk. But now you and I are able to more calmly discuss things. We can compromise. I am so proud of us and how we can work things out. You are so easy to talk to now (SUPPORT).
>
> "I know it hasn't always been easy. You have worked really hard. You've changed so much how you deal with our relationship, even when I'm not at my best (EMPATHY). But compared to how we used to be, things go so much smoother. I feel like we are closer than ever" (TRUTH).

Keep an Opening

For some, total abandonment of the relationship will never occur. No matter how insulting and rejecting your child, parent, romantic partner, or other loved one may be, you may not want to irrevocably sever the connection. A sense of duty or responsibility, or of previous love or commitment, or of guilt may dictate a need to maintain some contact with a person whom, outside of your long-term connection, you would otherwise dislike and avoid. Even if the BP rejects you, despite your pain, you may wish to sustain some presence in his life.

The duty to keep the relationship may be agonizing if your loved one is constantly devaluing you. It takes great strength to fulfill your commitment. But you must maintain realistic expectations. You may never achieve the mutual, loving relationship you hope for. The connection may need to remain a distant one. You want to feel that you are trying your best to preserve some attachment without subjecting yourself to excessive abuse.

Accept the boundaries your loved one constructs. She will feel disrespected if you insist on sustaining a conversation she wants to end. Give her space, even if a misunderstanding remains unclarified for a time. If an interaction is too inflamed, don't try to immediately fix it. If the BP angrily hangs up on you, let time pass to cool down.

Remember a birthday or special occasion with a card or short call acknowledging the event. Accept that there may not be any appreciation or even recognition of your efforts. Don't use any contact to be defensive or resurrect another argument. Instead, steel yourself against the BP's disdain and try to keep open a window that someday may result in some acceptable reconciliation. In the meantime, concede the distance she maintains.

"What's Love Got to Do with It?"

There are many reasons to hold on to a loving but tumultuous relationship. You are strongly attached to someone for whom you care deeply. You have worked hard to maintain the relationship, even through difficult times. You have adapted to many challenges and explored better ways to cope.

But if the connection is too exhausting, if it is threatening your own health, you need to evaluate your reasons for staying. And some of the reasons you give, or receive, by themselves, may not be good enough.

- *"But I still love her!"* may not be enough to sustain an intimacy in which you continue to be pummeled. It takes more than love to sustain a healthy partnership.

If you are continuing to suffer in the relationship, your love will ultimately be drained.

- *"But what will happen to him if I leave?"* expresses your concern that the BP will regress or maybe be unable to survive if you withdraw. You may feel guilty, and he may bolster those feelings by condemning you for your heartless abandonment. But if you are satisfied that you have provided your "best shot," you should not be deterred. The change may actually strengthen the BP, forcing him to be more responsible. However, if he is truly unable to develop insight into his problems and work on them, your attempted interventions may only postpone inevitable decline. Hanging on longer might eventually result in a more precipitous collapse when the relationship inevitably ends.

- *"For the sake of the kids"* or the effects on others is a consideration if the connection dissolves. How children will deal with splitting up must be evaluated. However, their exposure to the conflicts between the adults may be worse if you stay. Disapproval from others does not justify your unhappiness.

- *"Can we at least be friends?"* may reflect your loved one's sincere wish or desperate attempt to maintain the relationship. After any intimate connection has ended, it is hard to sustain the relationship on a different level. The BP views many things in extremes of black or white, one way or the other. The nuance of shifting from lover to friend may be difficult to navigate. If you do wish to maintain some connection, you must clarify its boundaries for both of you. This may include agreeing on how often you will communicate, how physically intimate you will be, and what your responsibility will be to her. If these boundaries prove porous, you may find yourself pulled back into the same unhealthy relationship you were trying to modify.

Know When to Walk Away

There will be times when the challenges of maintaining the relationship may become overwhelming. You will want to determine if a satisfying future can be obtained. When considering whether to end the connection, you will first want to carefully evaluate if there is likely to be progress in the relationship. In these situations progress is highly unlikely:

- After years of individual and couples therapy, he persistently blames you for any conflict. He will assume no responsibility for the friction between you.

- He becomes angry and refuses further contact with any professional who tries to point out his contribution to troublesome interactions.

- The dysfunction in the relationship has remained fixed. Over time you see no change or likelihood of change.

- Suspicion and paranoia continuously infect the relationship. Trust cannot be established even after years together and with adequate professional intervention.

- Threats or violence hinder your personal safety.

- The emotional pain of leaving is less than the persistent and unchanging pain of staying.

Know When to Stay

The decision to stay with your loved one is not a passive acquiescence. It is an affirmation that you foresee a healthy future together. This commitment is made over time with much thoughtfulness. You want to consider the signs that both of you are working toward the same long-term goals:

- You both can "get past" an argument, not by ignoring it, but by either compromising or agreeing you can disagree and remain mutually respectful.

- You value your current intimacy more than the prospect of a different relationship or solitude.

- You feel your relationship is improving.

- You care deeply for this person, and she is motivated to stay connected to you too.

- She is someone who, despite certain upsetting behaviors, exhibits admirable, endearing qualities that you value.

- She recognizes that she struggles with problems and is trying to alleviate them.

- There is evidence she is sincerely working with you on the relationship and is making progress.

For many people, a satisfying relationship with another is an important part of what determines a meaningful and contented life. Maintaining intimacy with others, especially those with emotional burdens, is challenging. You have chosen to pursue love that may push you, resist you, even hurt you. Your courage and strength is reflected in your commitment to be with and support the person you love.

This book has aimed to provide a framework that can improve your relationship with someone who exhibits behaviors suggestive of BPD. Both you and the one you love have the opportunity and the right to be happy. Hopefully, some of what is reflected in these pages can help you and your loved one work together to achieve the contentment you both deserve.

Resources

Publications

Chapman, Alexander, and Kim Gratz, *The Borderline Personality Disorder Survival Guide* (Oakland, CA: New Harbinger Publications, 2007).

Friedel, Robert O., *Borderline Personality Disorder Demystified: An Essential Guide for Understanding and Living with BPD*, rev. ed. (Boston: De Capo Press, 2018).

Gunderson, John G., and Perry D. Hoffman, *Understanding and Treating Borderline Personality Disorder: A Guide for Professionals and Families* (Washington, DC: American Psychiatric Publishing, 2005).

Kreisman, Jerold J., and Hal Straus, *I Hate You—Don't Leave Me: Understanding the Borderline Personality*, 2nd ed. (New York: Perigree, 2010).

Kreisman, Jerold J., and Hal Straus, *Sometimes I Act Crazy: Living with Borderline Personality Disorder* (Hoboken, NJ: John Wiley & Sons, 2004).

Manning, Shari Y., *Loving Someone with Borderline Personality Disorder* (New York: Guilford Press, 2011).

Mason, Paul, and Randi Kreger, *Stop Walking on Eggshells*, 2nd ed. (Oakland, CA: New Harbinger Publications, 2007).

Websites

Black Sheep Project (a community designed to connect those dealing with BPD): https://www.blacksheepproject.org

BPD Central (resources, including books and articles): http://www.bpdcentral.com

BPD Family (coping tools for families): http://www.bpdfamily.com

BPD Recovery (for individuals recovering and seeking help): http://www.bpdrecovery.com

BPD Resource Center (general information for individuals and families): http://www.bpdresources.net

National Education Alliance for Borderline Personality Disorder (support and education for relatives, consumers, and professionals): https://www.borderlinepersonalitydisorder.com

National Institute of Mental Health (fact sheets and general information): https://www.nimh.nih.gov/health/topics/borderline-personality-disorder/index.shtml

Treatment and Research Advancements for BPD (support center that educates and fights stigma): http://www.tara4bpd.org

Blogs

Healthy Place: More Than Borderline: https://www.healthyplace.com/blogs/category/borderline/

Psychology Today: http://www.psychologytoday.com/experts/jerold-j-kreisman-md

Jerold J. Kreisman, MD, is a psychiatrist and leading expert on borderline personality disorder (BPD). He is coauthor of the best seller *I Hate You—Don't Leave Me*, which is considered a classic of both the popular and academic literature on BPD, and has been completely revised and updated in 2010. His book *Sometimes I Act Crazy* describes how families and friends confront the disorder. Kreisman produces a blog for *Psychology Today*. He lectures widely in the United States and abroad, and is in private practice in St. Louis, MO.

Foreword writer **Randi Kreger** is creator of the website www.bpd central.com and the Welcome to Oz online support community. She is coauthor of *Stop Walking on Eggshells*, and speaks and gives workshops about BPD internationally.

FROM OUR PUBLISHER—

As the publisher at New Harbinger and a clinical psychologist since 1978, I know that emotional problems are best helped with evidence-based therapies. These are the treatments derived from scientific research (randomized controlled trials) that show what works. Whether these treatments are delivered by trained clinicians or found in a self-help book, they are designed to provide you with proven strategies to overcome your problem.

Therapies that aren't evidence-based—whether offered by clinicians or in books—are much less likely to help. In fact, therapies that aren't guided by science may not help you at all. That's why this New Harbinger book is based on scientific evidence that the treatment can relieve emotional pain.

This is important: if this book isn't enough, and you need the help of a skilled therapist, use the following resources to find a clinician trained in the evidence-based protocols appropriate for your problem. And if you need more support—a community that understands what you're going through and can show you ways to cope—resources for that are provided below, as well.

Real help is available for the problems you have been struggling with. The skills you can learn from evidence-based therapies will change your life.

Matthew McKay, PhD
Publisher, New Harbinger Publications

If you need a therapist, the following organization can help you find a therapist trained in dialectical behavior therapy (DBT).

Behavioral Tech, LLC

please visit www.behavioraltech.org and click on *Find a DBT Therapist.*

For additional support for patients, family, and friends, please contact the following:

BPD Central Visit www.bpdcentral.org

Treatment and Research Advancements Association for Personality Disorder (TARA)
Visit www.tara4bpd.org

MORE BOOKS *from*
NEW HARBINGER PUBLICATIONS

**WHEN YOUR
DAUGHTER HAS BPD**

Essential Skills to Help
Families Manage Borderline
Personality Disorder

978-1626259560 / US $16.95

**STOP WALKING ON
EGGSHELLS,
SECOND EDITION**

Taking Your Life Back When
Someone You Care About Has
Borderline Personality Disorder

978-1572246904 / US $18.95

STRONGER THAN BPD

The Girl's Guide to Taking
Control of Intense Emotions,
Drama & Chaos Using DBT

978-1626254954 / US $16.95

**THE STOP WALKING ON
EGGSHELLS WORKBOOK**

Practical Strategies for Living
with Someone Who Has
Borderline Personality Disorder

978-1572242760 / US $25.95

THE WORRY TRICK

How Your Brain Tricks You into
Expecting the Worst & What
You Can Do About It

978-1626253186 / US $16.95

**THE BUDDHA &
THE BORDERLINE**

My Recovery from Borderline
Personality Disorder through
Dialectical Behavior Therapy,
Buddhism & Online Dating

978-1572247109 / US $18.95

newharbingerpublications
1-800-748-6273 / newharbinger.com

(VISA, MC, AMEX / prices subject to change without notice)

Follow Us 🛇

Don't miss out on new books in the subjects that interest you.
Sign up for our Book Alerts at **newharbinger.com/bookalerts**